What's Wrong with Work?

Praise for
What's Wrong with Work?

"The message is clear — what's right for people is right for the business."

John Timpson, Chairman, Timpson Ltd and author of Upside Down Management

"An excellent, practical guide to finding fulfilment at work. With the basic premise that the only person who can make you happy at work is yourself, and a focus on believing that change is possible, managers and anyone who works would do well to read this book."

Guy Clapperton, author of The Joy of Work? and This is Social Media

"If it is fast and lasting change you want, this is the book for you."

David Taylor, author of The Naked Leader books

"Insightful, smart and witty. Keep this book on your desk and refer to it daily."

Neil Mullarkey, founder of The Comedy Store Players

What's Wrong with Work?

The 5 Frustrations of Work and How to Fix them for Good

Blaire Palmer

A John Wiley & Sons, Ltd., Publication

Contents

Acknowledgements

It is wonderful to be able to publicly thank the people who have helped me write this book. I always wanted to be in the acknowledgements of someone else's book, thinking it would make me sound like I moved in artistic circles. I hope the people I am genuinely thanking here know how much I appreciate their hard work, their friendship and their advice, and that I really could not have done it without them. I also hope they get a little thrill from seeing their name in print.

Thank you to the managers who gave their time and their best tips for inclusion in *What's Wrong with Work?* – John Barnes, Paul Currah, Ian Hill, Belinda, Graham Massey, Karen Mellor and Jane Ginnever. Your combined 150 years of management experience was fascinating to hear about and, I am sure, will reassure and inspire managers who want to influence how their companies are run.

Thanks to my team at Taming Tigers – Jim Lawless, Aly Pendlebury, Julia Blower and Ros Munton, who have encouraged me, carved out time in my diary and left me alone when I needed to concentrate. Thanks also to the coaches and facilitators who inspire me and our clients – Pete Bernard, Ginny Baillie, Caroline

Gourlay, Sandra Lee, Dexter Moscow, David Pride, Katie Rowland, Rachel Turner and Neil Urquhart.

There are a few other people who have listened to me rage about what is wrong with work and, when I stopped for breath, offered helpful insights. They include Mike and Wendy Wilsher of the Executive Foundation, Ian Hughes of Consumer Intelligence, Ellen Hallsworth (my fabulous editor at John Wiley & Sons), Charlotte Howard (my brilliant agent), David Harris of Acorns 2 Oaks, Sam and Mike Harbord (my friends and opticians) and Catherine French of Revelation Events.

It is customary to thank your parents, but in my case it is particularly important as I wrote much of this book in their attic where I would not be disturbed, being refuelled occasionally with cups of Earl Grey and bowls of homemade soup. Thanks also to my sister Lindsey, who is also my best friend, for taking my calls and returning my voicemail messages at any time of the day or night.

Writing takes a great deal of time. I couldn't have found enough of that without the ongoing help and friendship of my au pair, Stephie Schliecker. And of course, lots of huggies and kisses to my daughter Ivy Belle who stops me taking myself too seriously.

Introduction: The 5 Frustrations of Work and How to Fix them for Good

A TYPICAL DAY AT THE OFFICE ...

It was five o'clock and we were all gathering for our meeting with the Editor. This meeting was crucial to the production of *Today*, BBC Radio 4's flagship news programme. It was always held very secretly so that none of the other BBC news programmes, produced out of the same large newsroom, could hear what we had planned for the next day's programme. Losing a top story to a competitor news organization was one thing. Losing a top story to a competitor programme in your own organization was unforgivable.

We had even, when we had a particularly juicy scoop, gone so far as to mislead other programmes about what our lead story was going to be by writing a total fabrication on our office whiteboard where we worked out the running order of the items on the show.

On this particular day, about 12 or 13 years ago, I had tried but failed to substantiate a series of stories I was working on. The job of a News Researcher in radio includes generating story ideas for the next day's programme and then trying to get someone in authority to come on the air, live, and speak about that story. Fingers crossed they get themselves in a pickle and say something inadvisable, which can then be repeated on the news bulletins throughout the day. That's how you really make your reputation and get promoted to Producer.

However, on this day, every story I was working on turned out to be untrue or the individual concerned was not convinced of the benefit of discussing it further with us. (I had heard some rumours and wanted to take them up directly with the people concerned, giving them a chance to set the record straight on live radio ... at least, that's how I sold the idea to potential guests when the reality was more like "Come on the radio and be badgered by one of our presenters for five minutes whilst a nation listens on". As a journalist, it is always very frustrating when the story turns out to be true but the individual concerned is a little too savvy to open themselves up to public ridicule, even when you've worked your tried and tested techniques on them for a good twenty or thirty minutes.)

I knew I was in for a hard time at the five o'clock meeting where the team members take turns to tell the Editor which guests they have lined up for the next day. When it came to me I explained that none of my stories could be substantiated so I had no guests, yet, for tomorrow's show. With three more hours of my 12-hour shift left there was time to rectify this situation, but we were getting towards the end of office hours for most people and finding interviewees at such short notice is challenging.

The Editor did not disappoint. He was furious in a quiet and menacing way. At the end of the meeting, armed with some new ideas, I headed back to my desk. A few minutes later the Editor reappeared and walked straight over to me. He put his hand on my back and whispered "You'd better fix someone for tomorrow's programme". As he walked away I felt something sticking to my jumper. I felt my back and discovered a Post-It my Editor had positioned there. It read:

"I am Satan's mistress"

Just before he closed the door to his office, he swung around and declared "Don't take that off until you have found someone for tomorrow's programme".

A newsroom is a rambunctious place. The hours are long, the pressure is intense. You are working towards hourly or daily deadlines and you cannot fail. The programme cannot go out on air with great silent gaps because you didn't find a decent story or because you had a tummy bug or because you were not "in the zone". I knew this, and much of the time I enjoyed the sense of being on the cutting edge of the news, knowing stories first, setting the agenda, being at the heart of the action. I have never laughed so much at work as I did in those days. When you are tired, stressed and a little afraid even averagely funny jokes become hysterical. Maybe, because we were all used to thinking fast, we were able to tap into a comedic talent we aren't able to access when we are more relaxed and dopey. Or maybe things are just funnier when you are on the verge of a nervous breakdown.

However, I have also never cried so much as I did in that job. I would wake up with a bag of stones in my stomach, constantly waiting to be found out as a fraud. You were always judged on your last idea and, with a daily programme, you needed to have a great idea (and be able to back it up with a real-life studio guest) every shift.

At the time I believed that was what work had to be like. I had never really experienced anything different. I started working in the media during university, being paid a handsome £20 per week for producing a youth programme for a local radio station, and I didn't leave the industry until I was 30. My job was to get it right, to constantly prove I deserved to be there (because, as we were continually reminded, there were plenty of people who would give their right arm to do what we did), to avoid any personal controversy and to get a cubicle as far away from the Editor's office as possible.

THE FRUSTRATIONS OF WORK

My BBC career lasted about 10 years and, since leaving the BBC, I have had another 10 years' experience working inside large corporations, small owner-run businesses and everything in between as an executive coach and behavioural change expert. In that time I've listened to, participated in and observed thousands of hours of meetings, coaching sessions, workshops and briefings. And I have noticed that, no matter how different the industry, how different the setting, how different the personalities, the same patterns are repeated almost everywhere I go: endless meetings where nothing is discussed fully, where decisions are delayed and blame is assigned; unhealthy competition between teams and functions; a working hours culture which recognizes long hours over productivity; poor management and a lack of leadership; disengaged employees who work out of necessity not passion; compromised values and integrity; an inability to take bad news on board or learn from success or failure; the suffocation of promising ideas in favour of outdated and ineffective ways of doing things; and an absence of real vision.

The "Post-It Story", as it has become known amongst my friends, is a rare type of occurrence in the businesses I visit, verging on bullying in today's climate. And this book isn't about extreme behaviours by managers or the people they work with. But this story illustrates how we get so used to work being a difficult environment on occasion – and a place where we are fighting against obstacles daily in order to do our job well – that we forget to ask if it can be different.

Over the last decade I have noticed the ways organizations, and the individuals who work there, create or sustain barriers to success. And this isn't to say that the companies I have worked with are bad companies. Quite the contrary. They are amongst the best known and respected companies in the world. In all of them I find smart, ambitious, passionate, dedicated people who go above and beyond for their company, usually because they want to do a good job.

I meet junior members of staff who are keen to learn, who want to advance in the business and who have a variety of talents honed outside of work which they could bring to the company – people who run the local Scout group or who've climbed the world's highest peaks, or people who have lived abroad or make great cakes for family functions.

And I meet senior and more experienced members of staff who have made sacrifices for their organization, who have worked their way up to get to where they are today and who carry with them expertise they have developed over 10, 20, even 30 years and more.

But even in these great companies – companies which, like the BBC, have worldwide reputations for their products and services and strong brands where their name is seen as a sign of quality and reliability – I am struck by how much is not working well.

Despite their dedication, commitment and willingness to give, employees often feel under-valued and under-utilized. Whilst they enjoy "the day job", they have to put up with so much extraneous pressure that they are distracted from doing what they love and what they know. A scientist wants to focus on finding a cure for cancer but spends most of his time answering emails and attending meetings, a manager wants to invest energy in developing her people but instead spends her time fielding queries and wading through sales figures, a designer wants to take the briefing he has received from his client and use his creativity to bring it to life but spends his time trying to allay the fears of other stakeholders who are concerned about the risks of change.

These are the Frustrations of work. People rarely leave their job because they don't enjoy what they do. They leave (or want to leave) because of these Frustrations. When they complain about their job to their other half or to their buddies, it is these Frustrations they focus their energy on. It's the double-standard that tells them, on the one hand, that the customer is the number one priority but then specifies how long each customer service phone call can be in order to meet their target; it's the free work/life balance seminars held at lunchtime they can't attend because they can't afford to leave their desks for thirty minutes; it's the fact that they want to learn but can't risk showing their manager they don't understand something.

And yet, most of these Frustrations can be minimized or dispensed with altogether. Some companies have taken this very seriously and reinvented their workplace culture in order to slash the Frustrations their people need to endure. To give one example (there will be many more), let's look at what software company SAS does to minimize Frustrations. This company regularly features in the top 20 of the *Fortune* 100 Best Companies to Work For list and, in 2004, was celebrating 28 years of continual revenue growth. The company has medical facilities for employees and their dependents on site. It provides a Montessori day care centre and children are welcome in the company cafeteria so they can eat lunch with their parents. There is a fitness centre, which means employees can more easily stay healthy. There is a Work/Life Department, which helps employees find the best health care for their aging parents or find the right college for their children. Flexible workday guidelines encourage staff to start each day at whatever time is best for them. And people hold meetings because the situation demands it and not because "it's time".[1] The company believes that there are net gains financially to removing some of the Frustrations of work. The benefits not only make people more productive because they aren't distracted by thoughts like "How will I get to the gym today?" or "I feel guilty about my long working hours this week because I won't see my kids", but they help retain workers and therefore reduce the massive cost of recruitment and the cost of new employees who take time to get up to speed. People don't need to take off half a day to visit the doctor because the doctor is on site. And because the company subsidizes childcare, employees can afford to return to work because nursery school fees are low.

This isn't to say that employees in companies like SAS love every minute of their day and never have to handle difficult, boring or distracting situations. But, wherever possible, the obstacles to doing a great job and finding that job fulfilling and meaningful have been removed.

THE TIMES, THEY ARE A CHANGING ...

Today, people expect to do work which has meaning. Not only do we want to be protected from discrimination, from bullying and from inhaling other people's smoke, we want to be communicated with, given responsibility and receive regular pay rises and promotions. And, over and above that, we want our company to care about us and even about our lives outside of work (work/life balance, maternity and paternity leave, duvet days for instance).

Those expectations are on the rise. Today's recruits also want their employer to be socially responsible, offer flexibility and job security, and create a family-type atmosphere at work. One survey of Baby Boomers, Generation X-ers and Generation Y employees showed very strongly how expectations of work are changing as those born between 1979 and 1994 join the workforce and become increasingly influential.

86% of Generation Ys in the survey said they wanted to make a positive contribution to society and the health of the planet and that it was important that their work involve "giving back". (People in their 30s and early 40s are 10% less likely to find this important.) 89% of Generation Ys want flexible working options to be available and two-thirds want the opportunity to work remotely. A large number of Generation Ys (42% of women and 30% of men) say they talk to their parents every day and many are still financially dependent on their parents (which might explain the regular calls home!). Such reliance and close connection with family impacts the decisions these employees make about their career. They are less likely to seek work which offers huge financial reward if they can find work which has meaning for them. And 47% of Generation

Ys want their company to offer sabbatical leaves so they can pursue their interests outside of work without permanently giving up their jobs.

In fact, this research showed that the youngest and the oldest employees in your company have more in common with each other than with the Generation X-ers who were born between 1965 and 1978. If you are an X-er yourself, you might find it difficult to understand these newer recruits and assume it is simply their youth which informs their work style and their values. This would be a mistake. These younger employees will hold on to their values throughout their working life, just as the Baby Boomers have held on to theirs. The research showed, for instance, that Boomers and Generation Ys often work together more effectively than either group work with Generation X employees, even if there are many layers of hierarchy between them.[2] If you are Generation X and you manage Generation Ys you may well notice that you are often bypassed as your direct reports head straight for your line manager.

If you are a Generation Y employee yourself, a lot of this may resonate with you. For you, the challenge is to bring about changes in the culture of your organization despite the pressure from above to become more like your line manager (probably a Generation X-er). Your instinct will tell you the times are changing, and what worked yesterday won't work tomorrow. But you will face barriers to change, just like every generation of employees before you.

Whilst the Generation Y requirements might seem to be nice-to-haves to their (Generation X) bosses, there is also a growing body of evidence that they make financial sense too. In research by

Hay Group, highly engaged employees were found to improve business performance by up to 30%. Fully engaged employees are 2.5 times more likely to exceed performance expectations than their "disengaged" colleagues.[3]

THE BOW TIE EFFECT

So, who is responsible for creating better companies which make more money? Who can stop work being boring, frustrating, stressful, unhealthy, unfulfilling, limiting and meaningless?

You.

As a manager in your business you sit in a pivotal position, able to cause a ripple effect in your organization if you choose to do so.

There are three ways you can do this. The first is that you can make work more meaningful for you personally. You do this by changing the way you see yourself, others, the company you work for and the world at large.

The second is that you manage people differently. You do this by changing the way you see yourself, others, the company you work for and the world at large.

The third is that you change your organization from the inside. You do this by changing the way you see yourself, others ... Am I getting boring yet?

So it's simple, isn't it? Except that what I am suggesting is the most difficult job you have as a manager. Whether you have done a great deal of self-development and professional development before or whether this is the first time you have sought some answers to your management questions, changing the way you view your reality is tough and, I am sorry to say, a never-ending process.

No matter how dedicated you are to changing yourself and changing the situation you find around you, you will never get to the point where you see everything clearly and have no further need to challenge your perceptions. Every situation you encounter is going to be a little different and require a fresh approach. Every stage in your career is going to throw up new challenges, which means you need to reassess the lessons you have learnt to date. Every new generation of employees entering the business is going to have different values and demands and you need to move with the times.

And it is this concept of continual relearning which makes or breaks management careers. Those managers who are open to learning, who question their assumptions continually and who are curious to understand the other person's point of view enjoy their work more, bring out the best in others, and are catalysts for change in their organization and beyond.

Those managers who believe they know it all or believe they must been seen as all-knowing, who stop asking questions and listening to other people, and who carry their beliefs around without ever questioning their value obstruct the contribution of other people, get in the way of vital change in their organization and find work a struggle.

The job of middle management is a much misunderstood and undervalued one. Most managers, even if they or their direct reports see them as quite senior, are middle managers in reality. They have managers above them and managers below. It is what John Barnes, one of the managers I interviewed for this book, called "The Bow Tie Effect".

Middle managers are literally stuck in the middle. They are blamed when information from the top does not filter down and when information from the bottom does not filter up. They are often perceived by those below and above as competitive, protectionist and threatened by more talented people. They are the easy scapegoats when an organization is losing money, losing people or losing its way. And they are seen, as much as anything, as a talent pool from which the future leaders of the organization will be plucked. They are not appreciated in their own right as the grease that oils the wheels of the business, the coaches, advocates and teachers, the individuals with the power to transform the culture of the company, and even the lives of the people who work for them.

If you are a middle manager you have far more influence than you may realize. On a daily basis you may feel quite powerless and that your only option is to work within the system or leave the system. But in the pages of this book you will hear from many managers who have chosen an alternative – to bring about change from the middle of the organization. Some have done this in small ways, barely perceptible to anyone else (except that their team is the best performing in the business). Some have brought about radical change, impacting the company culture far beyond their own team or function.

And successful managers see this as their job. It isn't what they do in their own time. They don't feel they are paid to meet their targets and, as a hobby, they take an interest in their people and the way their organization is run. They see this as a fundamental part of their job. They recognize that change is a fact of life and they don't only want to be swept along by that change, but to influence and even direct it. They want to leave behind a legacy which is more than just the share price on the day they retired or their portrait in the boardroom (if companies even do that these days).

5 AREAS OF FOCUS

I believe (and I am not alone) that there is a cultural change going on, fed by the recent recession but also by concerns about the environment, work/life balance, ethics and high-profile corporate scandals. People are looking for a way to love their work and challenge the prevailing corporate culture. As middle managers you hold the key to this transformation.

This can feel like an overwhelming task. Where do you start? Is there a thread which you can unpick and the whole of corporate life as we know it will unravel? There might be (the quake pulsating through the world money markets in the wake of the near-fatal failure of the banking industry could have been such a thread), but that isn't what you want to do, is it? You just want work to work better for you, for your colleagues and for the business itself.

It is more fruitful to focus on a small number of key areas which, in most businesses, constitute Frustrations. I have identified a shortlist of 5 common factors which I have seen in numerous businesses over the last decade, and which many of my clients have tinkered with (or redesigned wholesale), which get you the biggest bang for your buck.

This is backed up by other research on the subject, including the *Sunday Times* 100 Best Companies to Work For survey, research by Hay Group, Harvard Business School and others showing that fixing a small but crucial (and in some instances obvious) set of problems in a business can transform the experience of working there and the results the business achieves.

In each case, I have given ideas about how you can shift your beliefs about yourself in relation to that issue, how you can manage other people more effectively around that issue, and how you can bring about a more widespread change with regard to that issue which impacts the organization beyond your team.

This isn't a "How To" book though. In every business, every function and every team the exact problem will be unique. It is ultimately up to you and those around you to choose or design the steps necessary in order to address the Frustration as it appears in your business. This book will give you some ideas about alternative ways of seeing the problem and start you off with some solutions that have worked well for other managers in other businesses.

Frustration 1: Waste-of-Time Meetings. One of the biggest bug-bears of corporate life is meetings. On average, professional people spend 60 hours a month in meetings, about a third of their working time. Many, of course, spend significantly more time eating bourbon creams, drinking dishwater coffee and composing their shopping list while someone else wades through a 30-slide business case for Dress Down Fridays. If it is accurate, as one study found, that 30–50% of time in meetings is wasted, it isn't surprising that most of us feel we could be utilizing this time better. The question is, what is a better way to share information, make decisions and review progress? In this section I reveal where most meetings go wrong, and how you can make the most of a room full of brainpower.

Frustration 2: Mis-Leadership. It isn't leadership that is the Frustration, it is lack of leadership. And lack of decent management too. You may have noticed that I have been referring to "managers" throughout this Introduction, instead of "leaders". That is partly because "middle leaders" isn't a recognized title whereas "middle managers" is. It is also because

I want to explore with you what these terms – manager and leader – actually mean. There is certainly a connotation that leaders are better than managers. Everyone wants to call themselves a leader now. But there is a great deal of research on the role and importance of managers which is useful to understand before you decide whether you are a leader or a manager or, step back in shock, both. The bottom line is that very few people are good at either let alone both of these disciplines, and this section will explore what tomorrow's leader-managers or manager-leaders could look like.

Frustration 3: Blurred Vision. Most companies will claim to have a vision. They may have spent a great deal of money identifying that they value "Passion, quality and results" or that they aim to be "Fast, effective and forward-thinking" or that they exist to "Put people first". The members of the board will argue that they know why they are here – "To make money and be Number 1 in our market". And leaders will cite the financial targets for this year as the focus of all their activity. In reality, most people don't know why their company is better (or even if it is better) than the competition. They don't know what the company values are (or if they do, they don't see them reflected in the behaviour of their colleagues). And they don't know how their daily toil contributes (or if it does contribute) to the success of the business. Whilst middle managers can rarely influence the vision of their organization as individuals (unless the company is genuinely seeking their input), they can understand the need for context. When they communicate, how they communicate, what they stand for ... all of these can become a kind of vision. Most of us don't need to know what the company stands for if we know how we fit in to the team or function in which we work. You can learn to be a visionary manager whether you then bring about massive cultural change in your business or not, and some clues about how to do that are given in this section.

Frustration 4: Silo Mentality. How long is it going to be before companies stop talking about the dangers of "silo" working and start doing something about it? Whether it is competition between different offices in the same business, wariness between functions or downright hatred between teams, most companies ignore or unintentionally support the factions within their business. Companies are not like production lines, where those at one end of the line have nothing to say to those at the other end. They are interconnected organisms which require every part of the business to be working with every other part of the business. If you've ever struggled to get answers from another part of your company, don't know who anyone is outside of your own team, or feel in direct competition with your colleagues, you are at the sharp end of the silo mentality. What is the cost of such division and can't we all just live together as one big happy family?

Frustration 5: Unfairness. A complaint I hear regularly when I spend time in other businesses is that work isn't fair. Many of us have been appalled by the recent stories of MPs' perks, the extravagances of Wall Street financiers and the behind-the-scenes goings on at high-profile failing businesses. And yet we shouldn't really be so surprised. We know from our own experiences of work that we are often asked to behave in ways which conflict with our values – we find ourselves having to be rude or pushy just to get the job done, and we have to redefine lying as "being economical with the truth" (or we have to sit by while our colleagues behave this way and are rewarded for it). But today's employees find it more and more distasteful to compromise their sense of what is fair. Increasingly, people won't work for companies who don't have admirable values. Attracting the best people, then, requires you to be an upstanding company. And that requires you to be an upstanding person. In this section I look at how you keep your sense of integrity when the temptation to fiddle the numbers, pass the buck or just keep your mouth shut while someone else takes the fall is so powerful.

FROM THE MANAGER'S MOUTH

Over the years I have worked with many managers who have taught me more about what's wrong with business and how to fix it than I could ever get from reading management books or attending leadership seminars. I have often wished I could get these mentors, friends and colleagues in a room together and tap all their wisdom, experience and insights so that I could share what they have to offer with a wider audience. These are individuals who have been on a journey of growth throughout their management career, who are curious about how they get in their own way, and who have developed strategies to minimize the problems they create, perpetuate or notice around them. Some started as coaching clients of mine or key contacts during organizational culture change programmes I have led. Others are colleagues whom I have worked with as peers. They are all people who have influenced my thinking and my professional development.

I think it is really valuable to listen to managers from other industries with different experiences from your own in order to keep an open mind about how problems can be resolved. It is hugely useful to know what questions managers have asked themselves in order to continually improve their performance. And, rather than reinventing the wheel, it is helpful to know how other people have influenced seemingly impossible situations and follow the same successful process yourself. That's why organizations like the Executive Foundation (of which I am on the board), the Academy for Chief Executives and Vistage have been created, bringing leaders together to share expertise, give advice and challenge assumptions. It is why many organizations encourage their own managers to network or choose a mentor from outside their company. New ideas are generated when seemingly unrelated concepts collide, so when you bring people with different perspectives, expertise and experiences together something fresh is more likely to be created.

And this is why I have spoken to some of the wisest managers I have ever worked with to elicit their stories, suggestions and insights, and share them with you. Within these pages you will read how they have overcome some of the hurdles you face, how they continue to struggle and seek answers to some of the questions you may have posed, and what shifts in attitude they have made, for better or worse, in order to achieve their current level of success.

None of these individuals is the finished article. They are each a work in progress. Don't trust anyone who claims to have all the answers! None of them believes they are expert at resolving the Frustrations explored in this book. My intention, though, is that some of their experiences resonate with you and that they provide food for thought as you tackle the most significant Frustrations in your workplace.

In addition to their insights, and my own drawn from years of experience deep inside a vast array of different types of business, I will share some of the research by other authors and experts in relevant fields. It is the same material that I often share with my own coaching clients and with organizations I am helping through the culture change process, and which will provide you with data, case studies and reassurance as you start to tackle What's Wrong with Work.

First, though, let's think about why you would want to.

When Work Works

> "I think I am in my dream job at the moment. I want to feel I am making a difference and in this job I do. Being able to make that difference has a massive impact on my well being, my life satisfaction. I really feel we are going to achieve our ambitions and that is a fantastic goal to aim towards."
>
> Jane Ginnever, HR Manager

Wouldn't it be great to be able to say that about your job? To wake up every day looking forward to the challenges ahead, even though they may be tough? But what does it take to feel that way about your work? What kind of company succeeds in creating a culture where work is a joy? And why would those companies bother to prioritize staff happiness?

If we were able to fix everything that is wrong with work, work could really work for us. It could provide us with meaning and fulfilment of the kind Jane describes. It could bring us happiness and a sense of worth. Clearly, that would be great for us as individuals. But the question remains – why would our employer care?

In this chapter I hope to get you excited about how work could be a more fulfilling and enjoyable experience for you and your colleagues, and explain why this is good for business. The rest of the book will focus on specific areas of work which could really benefit from a shake-up and give you some ideas about how to bring about change in small or dramatic ways. But unless you can picture what a great working environment would look like, and convince yourself that such a working environment is achievable and desirable, the advice in this book will simply strike you as naïve and unrealistic.

In addition, you may need to question some of your deeply held beliefs about work and understand some of the deeply held beliefs that your senior managers may hold about work. Bringing about change in yourself, others and organizations starts with challenging beliefs and assumptions. If beliefs and assumptions are left unquestioned, and change is simply pasted on top of old foundations, it won't stick. So in this chapter I will also reveal one of the fundamental assumptions that prevents work from really working and offer an alternative perspective.

THE ARGUMENT AGAINST A "HAPPY" WORKFORCE

Every year the *Sunday Times* newspaper publishes a list of the 100 best companies to work for. Businesses are scored against eight criteria which, through extensive research, are shown to measure "employee engagement" (or what used to be called "job satisfaction"). It isn't the only survey of its kind, but it is one of the most high profile. The top 100 get the positive exposure that comes with being at the top of a league table that is read nationwide. The rest take part because they want to compare themselves with the best employers in the country.

It is easy to see how getting a high score in an employee engagement survey might indicate that a company was a fun place to work. After all, if your company had inspirational leaders, exceptional line managers, opportunities to grow, manageable levels of stress, a good team spirit, a sense of corporate responsibility, a buzz amongst the employees and fair pay and benefits you would probably have little to complain about too.

But would a good score necessarily mean your company was successful? Whilst instinct might tell us that it must, it is worth considering the possibility that it doesn't. This is because, if you plan to bring about changes to the way you work and the way those around you work, you are likely to face opposition. You may be attacked by those who have a lot to lose by changes in the status quo. And the very concept of creating a happier workforce by resolving some of the Frustrations of work will be ridiculed.

Let's look at the criticisms some might level at employee engagement surveys and the assumptions that the Pro-Employee Brigade make.

Firstly, surveys like this do not ask about traditional "success factors" such as the achievement of targets or the financial well-being of the company. So one could suggest that, whilst we all want to enjoy our work, the findings are of little interest if your primary focus is profitability. And, after all, if a business doesn't make any money it cannot provide work of any kind for its employees, let alone enjoyable and meaningful work.

An argument that I often hear when I start working with companies is that one must balance the needs of employees against the needs of the business. There is a belief that companies who focus on employee engagement inevitably compromise on profitability. And, whilst employee engagement is nice to have, it cannot be more important than focusing on numbers like sales figures, overhead costs and share price.

Secondly, the questions in these surveys are all about perception not reality. Employees are asked how they *feel*. And feelings are subjective. One person might be earning £100,000 a year and feel unhappy with their pay. Another might earn £25,000 and feel happy with their pay. So, again, one could argue that the results of such a survey don't tell us whether the company has got these issues right. They only tell us how people feel about these issues. And you can't please all of the people all of the time, can you?

Thirdly, employees are not asked about their own performance but the performance of everyone else. Surely such a survey creates a climate of blame. We can just hear lazy, good-for-nothing layabouts blaming all their problems on their manager, or their team mates, or the HR department for not training them properly, can't we?

And finally, they are all about soft skills. Where are the questions about quality of product? Where are the questions about technical ability? Companies compete on quality and price, not on who has the happiest staff. It doesn't much matter if people enjoy their work if the product is shoddy and no one wants to buy it.

These questions and concerns are common. Conventional thinking has it that issues like corporate social responsibility and employee well-being are costly distractions from the main purpose of business – to make money. And particularly when the economy is wobbly and the prevailing culture is one of caution, spending money on creating a happier workforce without a guaranteed return on investment does not appeal to any but the most risk-tolerant leader.

In a way, it isn't surprising that the leaders of these companies are sceptical about employee engagement. As far as they are concerned, they have some much more pressing matters to attend to before they start thinking about a happy workforce. Let me explain. A company normally decides it needs a radical rethink about how it runs its operation when it has been successful financially for a number of years but continuing that level of growth is becoming harder than ever before. Typically, at about this time, the senior leadership team look around their business and notice levels of absenteeism are increasing. There is higher staff turnover. Recruitment costs are spiralling. Silos are starting to develop. And the senior management team itself, which used to work so well together, is now bickering and back-stabbing.

All of this hits the bottom line. Losing people costs far more than the recruitment costs alone. When people start losing interest in their work they start to slacken off. Before they eventually leave they become what I call "the walking dead". They are there in body but they contribute very little. This attitude can be infectious, leading to performance issues with other people on the team. They take up more of their manager's time, meaning he or she is achieving less. And when "the walking dead" do eventually leave and someone new is recruited it takes them time to get up to speed. All of this is expensive for a business.

When the top team starts to fracture that has a cost too. Instead of speaking openly about problems in their part of the business, they start sweeping issues under the carpet. They don't feel confident to share dilemmas because they may be perceived as vulnerable in an environment where there are low levels of trust. What starts as a small issue that would be simple to resolve if the team worked together can escalate into an insurmountable problem which eventually comes to everyone's attention anyway and dominates every meeting of the senior managers. We've all been there, haven't we? Meetings where subjects are avoided and people aren't confident about expressing their honest opinions. And we know that, as a result, real issues are not being addressed properly and a disaster is inevitable.

Because all of this starts to show up in the bottom line there is only one option available to the leadership, as far as they are concerned. Push harder. The costs of running the business have risen so they need to make more money. They need their staff to work harder to achieve ever-increasing targets. They need people to stay late and work at the weekend in order to keep up with their projects. They need to push their sleeves up and get on with the task rather than "wasting time" discussing the long-term strategic vision or investigating creative solutions to underlying problems. And, until they can sort out these urgent priorities, all the employee engagement stuff will have to wait.

What is the effect of this approach? Levels of stress increase, morale decreases, staff turnover grows, the tensions between different parts of the business become more pronounced, which means costs increase still further. So the company looks at some other ways to save money. Perhaps it outsources parts of its operation to a cheaper market. Or it makes redundancies (or "efficiencies" as they are also known), meaning the overhead cost decreases but so does the company's capacity to achieve its ambitious targets. Some companies start measuring the activity of their staff – how long they spend on a phone call, how many hours they are at the office, how many sick days they take. Others focus on share price – if the stock has gone up in value today they are happy, if it has gone down then drastic action must be taken. To me it's like being on a diet and weighing yourself after every meal to see if you've lost any weight yet or whether you're allowed to have pudding.

Can you see where all of this is heading? In exactly the opposite direction to that intended. The company wanted to grow and now it is cutting jobs and moving its operation to Taiwan. And this isn't a dramatized version of events. I have simply described what I have seen. And maybe you know this is the reality because you have experienced it too. Maybe you are experiencing it today.

But in such a climate, any talk of executive coaching for leaders, exploring corporate values, developing a strong leadership brand, improving the well-being of staff, investing in corporate social responsibility projects, setting aside time to develop people and give them opportunities outside the strict confines of their own role is put on the back burner. "We'll do that when we are through this crisis" is the common response.

It is easy to see how the value of employee engagement, even the value of people, takes a low priority when the focus is all on overhead and stock valuation. And in such an environment there is certainly a strong argument that whilst a happy workforce is nice to have, it can't be a priority.

This is a scenario that is familiar to Jane Ginnever, whom we heard from earlier. She is HR Manager with a successful and fast-growing property company. She joined the business when the company CEO and MD decided to address some of the simmering issues in their business:

"The company has grown very quickly and we're on the [*Sunday Times*] Fast Track 100 listing again this year. But we are feeling some repercussions of the strategy that has been used to build so quickly. We've seen a short-term focus, tightly controlled costs, little investment in people development and HR practices and little emphasis on getting the right people in to the right posts. HR as a function has only really been in existence within this company for about 2 years. Where we are trying to get to is a company with a much longer-term, sustainable future. There will be further growth inevitably but we want to bring people in to the group in the right way in future."

THE FLAWED ASSUMPTION

If your company is struggling with these problems, it doesn't mean it is "bad". What companies like this are experiencing is just part of the lifecycle of a growing business. Every company faces the same tensions as they approach milestones in their existence. Those who get through this phase are those who address the problems. Those who don't face up to the fact that they are in a counterproductive spiral rarely come out of it in one piece. See it as a mid-life crisis if you wish. Companies who see mid-life as an opportunity to reinvent themselves and live up to a more mature and fulfilling set of values find there is life after 40. Those who ignore what is happening to them find themselves back in bedsit-land having blown everything they had on fast cars and designer gear in order to maintain the illusion of youth.

What is also important to remember, before we blame senior management for all the ills of the workplace, is that there is nothing wrong with the motivations of the senior team. They want to grow. They want to create capital. They want to employ more people. They want to get their products out into the world. There is nothing innately anti-employee or anti-happy workplace about these ambitions. But it can certainly feel like it when you are lower down the hierarchy, feeling that the working environment isn't working for you.

Ian Hill is a middle manager with an international technology company. It's a challenge he has experienced at times early in his career:

"You are caught like the meat in a sandwich, managing up and down. You know what is right by the team and what should be done but there is a clear message from up high that you are not able to do that. For instance, when you are thinking about keeping staff during difficult times you can see the long-term impact on your group is immense but the message from above is that someone has to go.

You know the people who work for you are going to be even more stretched to the detriment of their performance and their life. And you will lose your best people because they can find other jobs. And you are losing all that investment that has gone in to making them a really effective person. To jeopardize that for the sake of £20 or £30K seems ridiculous. There are probably other ways to make that saving."

And there are. But the obstacle to finding fresh, innovative, win/ win solutions which enable a business to grow without sacrificing the well-being of the people who work there is this assumption:

"You cannot reconcile what is right for the business with what is right for people."

We've all heard this before, haven't we? There is a powerful belief that if you do what is right for people, the business pays a price. And if you do what is right for the business, the people who work there pay a price.

I believe this assumption is fundamentally flawed. But assumptions and beliefs are powerful. If they remain unchallenged, they prevent us from seeing the world through different eyes. If we are not able to see the world through different eyes, we are not able to see new possibilities. We will continue to operate within a small set of tried and tested options, which don't work terribly well but are the only options we think we have.

To give you an example: If you have a personal assumption that bad things always happen to you, that assumption will be reinforced every time something bad happens. When something good happens you will either ignore it because it conflicts with your assumptions or see it as an aberration. Only by making a different assumption, for instance "Good comes from even the worst situation" can you start to generate a new set of options about how you could respond to disappointment, failure, missed opportunities or bad luck. Someone who assumes good always comes from bad would not be derailed by a failure but see it as an opportunity to grow. Someone who assumes good always comes from bad would be able to move on from disappointment and announce "Onwards and upwards". This would be far more difficult for the person who starts with a belief that, whatever they do, bad things always happen to them.

So if the corporate culture generally assumes that you have to choose between the well-being of the business and the well-being of the people it will, inevitably, choose the business.

However, some of the world's most successful businesses are challenging this old assumption about people and business and working with a new assumption:

"Only by doing what is right for people can we do what is right for the business."

They have realized that if they ignore the people aspect of their business, they miss the key to growing a successful company. To use the diet analogy again, they start focusing on what their body needs to be fit and healthy rather than obsessing about the scales.

What the *Sunday Times* list and other research reveals is that employees who find their work meaningful and enjoyable are willing to give that illusive discretionary effort. They will go the extra mile.

THE ARGUMENT FOR A "HAPPY" WORKFORCE

There has been a lot of research into the impact of a happy workforce on the success of a business, and I will share some of that with you now. The case is quite powerful.

According to Peter Warr and Guy Clapperton, authors of *The Joy of Work?*, happy people generally contribute more to an organization than their less happy counterparts: "More satisfied employees are likely to achieve more work goals. They will also be absent less often and remain with their organization for a longer time ... Satisfied workers have been shown to be more cooperative and supportive of colleagues, to provide stronger support to others in difficult times, and to be generally more willing to 'go the extra mile' for their colleagues".[1]

Marcus Buckingham and Curt Coffman helped to develop the Gallup Q12 questionnaire, which measures the strength of a workplace. However, they knew that they also needed to show that a strong workplace was also a productive workplace. They found that "those employees who responded more positively to the twelve questions also worked in business units with higher levels of productivity, profit, retention and customer satisfaction".[2]

You might say that it is understandable that employees in a better-performing company would be happier in their work than those in a worse-performing company, and that it isn't happiness which creates great results but great results which create happiness. However, Buckingham and Coffman also found that "employees rated the questions differently depending on what business unit they worked for rather than which company. This meant that, for the most part, these twelve opinions were being formed by the

employees' immediate manager rather than the policies and proce-
dures of the overall company."

This should be significant for you. It shows that it is the immediate manager who has the most influence on how people feel about
their work and not the company culture as a whole. It means that,
no matter how junior you are or how poor you feel your company
is at caring for its people, you can make a difference. And that difference will show up in your team's performance.

Another more recent survey published in the *Harvard Business
Review* showed that where CEOs focused primarily on maximizing
profit, employees developed negative feelings towards the organization. As a result, they were less willing to make personal sacrifices
for the company and, importantly, company performance was
poorer as a result. But when the CEO made it a priority to balance
the concerns of all the stakeholders – customers, employees, the
community, the environment – employees were more willing to
exert extra effort and company results improved.[3]

This growing body of evidence should reassure you as you begin
leading change in your organization. It isn't just our gut which tells
us that a positive company culture is good for business and good
for the people within that business, but hard evidence that there is
a strong link between performance and happiness at work.
Therefore, doing something about the Frustrations of the workplace makes sense not only from a human perspective but from
a business perspective. In fact, I would argue that you cannot
improve business unless you focus on people.

THE TROUBLE WITH "THE MIDDLE"...
AND THE OPPORTUNITY

One of the problems with most books about work, organizational change and leadership is that they assume you can, single-handed, change your company. In reality, being a middle manager can feel like the least powerful place to sit in the hierarchy.

John Barnes is a General Manager for a large manufacturing company. He has an imaginative analogy to summarize the quandary of middle management:

> "You have to try to understand the knitting pattern your senior managers are working with and you have to ensure that their knitting pattern interfaces with the one you are using. This ensures that the final decision is recognizable to both parties. That's because their knitting pattern will often interfere with what you are trying to do if they don't realize what you are trying to do."

One of the managers I spoke to admitted, off the record, that he felt the agenda at the top of the business was different from the agenda lower down and that this creates a conflict which lands squarely on middle managers to resolve:

> "At the top decisions are tied to the stock value and things like that. I think senior managers believe the stock value reflects their own value, not just the value of the company, so they become focused on the short-term
>
> *Continued*

financial number. You can't just have increased dividends every year. That must come to an end at some point. But people get on that treadmill and no one wants it to be 'on my watch'. That's their agenda rather than the agenda of the person lower in the organization who is more focused on meeting customer needs. There is a genuine clash of agendas."

If this is the reality, then your chance to make a difference is rather limited isn't it? Well, no. Both John and the other manager quoted, despite the very real challenges they experience as they work their way up their organizations, have brought about changes in their own part of their businesses by changing their own perspective and, consequently, changing the perspectives of the people around them. Sometimes those changes have had a wider impact. Sometimes they have just affected the people in their immediate sphere. But, as we saw earlier, it is our relationship with our direct manager which has the greatest influence on our attitude to our work and therefore our productivity.

As a manager of people you greatly influence the work experiences of the people who report to you. Whether intentionally or not, your attitudes, perceptions and behaviour impact the performance of others. And when you change your attitudes, perceptions and behaviour you change the culture – the feel – of the place you work.

Fiat CEO, Sergio Marchionne, understood this. His task was to turn a company which had been a laughingstock in the industry into brand leader. He decided to challenge what he called "The

Great Man" model of leadership and create a culture where everyone was expected to lead. Instead of seeing his own job as making all the decisions about the business, he saw his job as setting challenging objectives and helping managers work out how to reach them.[4] This approach also reflected his natural style of leadership. Rather than conforming to a model of leadership which didn't feel right or natural to him, he rethought what a leader needed to be and created a new culture in his company, based on a more authentic, democratic leadership style.

You aren't CEO, yet. But you can redefine what being a leader requires of you. Does it mean you need to know the answers? Or does it mean you need to know the questions? Does it mean you have to push and cajole? Or does it mean you mentor and support? Are you the leader because you hold the title? Or are you the leader because people are willing to follow you? You get to decide the answers to these questions. You may not be able to challenge the behaviour of every manager in your business, but you can challenge your own and in doing that, you influence other people to do the same, just as Marchionne did.

IT'S ALL ABOUT YOU

The secret is out. Making work work isn't about changing your company. It is about changing yourself. Or let me put it a different way. It is about being true to yourself. Fixing what's wrong with work isn't about convincing others to do something differently or restructuring your team or even giving people more money and longer holidays. It is about identifying how work could really work for you and how you get in the way of that.

It is tough to concede that you may be part of the problem. I am not suggesting that you are the cause but that, unless you choose to challenge the status quo, you will find yourself condoning it.

You are working within a culture that has evolved and become entrenched, and you and your working environment are a product of that. The messages we were all given when we were growing up informed (and continue to inform) our attitudes to work. What were you told by parents, teachers and other influential adults?

"Make yourself indispensible"
"Please your teacher"
"Hand in your work on time"
"Work your way up the business"
"If you can't beat 'em, join 'em"

These seemingly sensible pieces of advice become beliefs and assumptions that influence our decisions, our attitudes and our behaviour. If you grew up being told to please your teacher, you will probably find it difficult to challenge your manager at work, to question his methods, to provide feedback to help him grow. If you were told you can't beat them so you might as well join them you may try to fit in, accepting how things are done in your company even though it seems counterproductive. If you were told to work your way up the business you may measure your success by how many promotions you have had rather than whether any of the changes you initiated stuck or whether your team grew in confidence and ability while you were their manager.

But the managers I have quoted in these pages have all chosen to question those beliefs and assumptions. They have chosen to resist the pressure to conform and, instead, tried to reinvent what being a manager means for them. They have taken into account the very real tensions that exist in the world of work and asked, not "What do I need to do?" or even "Who do I need to convince?" but "Who do I need to be in order to improve this environment?"

And why is it good for the business if you question conventional wisdom and work in a way that is true to yourself? Many people feel they have to leave a part of themselves at the revolving door of their company HQ when they arrive at work and pick it up again at the end of the day. I certainly felt like that when I worked at the BBC and have coached many successful people who, despite outward appearances, feel they must put on a suit of armour before entering their workplace in order to protect themselves, or hide their true selves, from the destructive influences of their office.

This strikes me as a terrible waste of potential. When you hide part of yourself you do not give your organization the opportunity to capitalize on everything you have to offer. What if some of the parts of yourself that you leave at the entrance could be of huge value to the company?

Graham Massey runs a consultancy which, in his words, "brings brand, people and business to life". He is passionate about the opportunity for companies to do good in the world by living up to high standards in everything they do. He feels that companies miss out when they ignore everything their employees could bring to the business:

"One problem is we don't look at people in the round. We take people on the basis of their CV and then we throw the CV away. We don't think 'You did a degree in marine biology' or 'You are interested in growing your own vegetables' or 'Didn't you do something on that 10 years ago?' I am sure there are people employed who are not using all their talents. You need to have the time and the culture in your business to say 'Blaire's got a degree in Mince Pies but she's here working with Sea Creatures. How do we make use of her ability to make Mince Pies?' Most employers will say they can't find the talent they are looking for. But they've already got people with latent talent. The problem is the attitude which says 'That's not your job' so we leave all that talent latent."

BACK TO THE 5 FRUSTRATIONS

There is a strong case to say that fixing what is wrong with work means that people are happier. (I don't mean that they are joyous every day and penalized for finding work challenging, tough, annoying or exhausting. But I do mean that their work brings them fulfilment and satisfaction and is a part of their life which makes them feel good deep down.) If people are happier there is evidence that they contribute more to the business and that is reflected in the bottom line. And there is ample argument that, wherever you sit in the company you work for, you can influence change by questioning outdated beliefs and assumptions about work and bringing everything you have to offer to your job as a manager.

But where do you start? Hopefully, knowing all of this is true provides you with a level of confidence so that you can start making some changes. But when so much is wrong, when the fundamental assumptions on which the world of work is based are flawed, what should be your priority?

The following 5 Frustrations are not in order of importance. They do not form a step-by-step action plan. However, if you can begin tackling the first – Meetings – you'll start creating some pretty impressive ripples in your company.

Frustration 1:
Waste-of-Time Meetings

"I think we should have footsteps on the floor"

This is the latest contribution from one of my potential new colleagues at a board meeting for trustees of a local art gallery. I have been invited to attend the meeting on the basis that, if I like it, I might become a trustee and help with the running and strategic planning of the art gallery, which is a few miles from my home in Wiltshire. But at this point in the meeting I have a strong sensation that joining this group of former teachers, yummy mummies and magistrates is going to be a mistake.

We have been sitting around the boardroom table for half an hour discussing how to ensure visitors see the whole gallery and don't get distracted by the sweet smell of chocolate brownies and thus spend most of their visit in the café. The only idea which has been proposed and is now being endlessly debated is placing little black footprint stamps on the floor showing patrons where to walk … and that those little black footprints take them to the upper floors of the gallery before leading them towards the gift shop and cappuccino.

The idea has excited everybody except me, it seems. I have tried to open up the debate to more ideas in the belief that (a) footprints are a bad idea and (b) we should come up with four or five ideas and then debate them, rather than debating one endlessly and never considering alternatives. However, I gave up my attempts to interrupt about 15 minutes ago and am now deciding what we are going to have for dinner and composing my shopping list.

Luckily for me, participation in this meeting in future is totally voluntary. When asked later whether I would like to join the board I politely decline. I am sure I can find better ways to spend my free time than in endless, waste-of-time meetings like this.

THE COST OF BAD MEETINGS

The subject matter of this particular meeting may not resonate with you but the frustration I felt – the lack of focus on important issues, the difficulty I found in participating, the obsession with one idea at the exclusion of potentially better ideas and the endless debate without decision – will all be familiar. And, unlucky for you, these meetings may be an everyday part of your working life and not an optional extra.

We spend, on average, 37% of our time in meetings.[1] Of that time, 30–50% is considered to be a waste of time. That means a typical person, working a 40-hour week, spends about 14 hours in meetings and 7 of those hours are totally wasted. That's approximately a day per week that contributes nothing to the business at all. And it isn't as if you are just twiddling your thumbs most weeks wondering how to fill your time. An extra day a week would come in very handy, wouldn't it?

Plus, meetings like the one I described have a hangover effect. Do you feel fired up and productive after a meeting like this? Are you confident that the right decision has been made? Are you able to take action when you leave because you are clear about the direction you and your team mates are all heading? Have the important issues been aired, or are there still "elephants in the room" which will continue to hamper your effectiveness?

Bad meetings impact how effective we are outside of the meeting. If a meeting is held but no decision is made, how can action follow? If people feel they are overlooked, attacked or ridiculed, how can they build trust amongst their colleagues? If a snap decision is made without the contribution of everyone in the meeting, how will the team react if that decision turns out to be flawed? Instead of accelerating and enhancing the work of the team members, bad meetings provide a huge obstacle to good performance.

But they also reflect the wider culture of the team or the organization as a whole. Bad meetings are a cause of bad work, but also an effect. If leaders in a company rarely praise their staff and regularly assign blame, you will see this played out in the company's meetings. If an organization is risk averse, you will find very little robust debate in its meetings. If people are valued for the number of hours they put in rather than their productivity, it is likely that meetings will be long and drawn out as yet more evidence of "how hard we all work".

And meetings are expensive. Not only is a company paying its people to spend a day a week achieving nothing, but it is incurring travel costs, sometimes catering costs and the cost of hiring rooms. It is paying for people to prepare for meetings, which takes them away from other activities. And none of this includes the lost opportunity cost.

Meetings should be the creative hub of a business. They should be where people get a grip on what is happening, how it affects them and the arguments in favour and against. They should be where people share their opinions and their expertise to ensure the best decision is taken. They should be a fast-track way of moving forward because all the right people are in the room at the same time and can avoid the braking effect of email communication. They should bring teams and work groups together, strengthening bonds and enhancing the sense of shared responsibility. They should be the places where the ideas are generated that save or make money for the business.

By and large, they don't do any of these things.

THE PROBLEM WITH MEETINGS …

Meetings in every organization are unique. The subject matter will depend on your industry and your role within that industry. A financial services marketing team meeting will be very different from a meeting of the IT department of a manufacturing site or a meeting between a salesperson and a potential customer.

But there are some common qualities of meetings which seem to cause most of the problems. They include:

1. The purpose and scope of the meeting is not defined.
2. Agendas are poorly designed.
3. The wrong people are present, the wrong people are absent.
4. People don't say what they really think.
5. No one knows what has been decided (or there is a disagreement about what has been decided).
6. Decisions made at meetings don't stick.
7. The same issues come up again and again.
8. The need for consensus gets in the way of proper discussion.
9. Meetings are not creative and opportunities to do something better are missed.
10. Meetings are too "easy".

I can't guarantee that, if these 10 problems were resolved, you would spend less time in meetings. But if you resolved some of these problems you might not mind spending even more time in meetings. After all, if they were really productive, it would be worth a greater proportion of your time. It is possible to imagine that people working together could achieve far more than people slaving away in solitude. Get it right and you could be willing to spend far more time around the board table.

WHY DO PEOPLE PUT UP WITH BAD MEETINGS?

There are some attitude problems which have to be overcome if you are going to address the bad meeting culture in your team or organization. People have become accepting of bad meetings as a necessary evil. Few people have ever experienced a really good meeting so they assume it isn't possible to do things any other way. At the same time, they believe they can't miss a meeting or their commitment will be questioned, so they continue to attend meetings knowing that they have no value.

Meetings can even be seen as a break from "real" work. Some people attend because they will be seen to be doing something without having to really think or participate. General Manager, John Barnes, believes that making meetings "harder" would discourage time-wasters from attending and attract only those who really wanted to do some good work:

> "A badly run meeting is a rather relaxed place to be. You can sit back and not listen. It can be very passive. Meetings are less attractive if you know when you come out of the meeting a decision is made or an action is agreed, so now it is active. The more active meetings you can generate the more likely it is that only the people required will appear."

People also put up with bad meetings because they don't feel they can influence the meetings culture. Most of the meetings we attend aren't "ours". We haven't called them. We haven't invited the guests. We haven't been asked to contribute to the agenda. We don't even know how anyone else feels about the meeting, and wonder "If everyone else finds it hugely valuable who am I to question the structure?" Added to this, it may be your boss or your boss's boss who calls your worst meetings, and questioning their purpose might mark you out as a trouble-maker.

Karen Mellor has been a manager in the pharmaceutical industry for many years. She understands the problem all too well:

"You are invited to the meeting, you get there, you listen to 30 minutes of something totally different to what you came for and before you know it you have follow-on meeting after follow-on meeting. As an individual you can say 'Can we have some structure?' But if the meeting is called by someone more senior anyone will find it difficult to say that. And the more senior the person the less time they probably have to put in to the structure."

If you are going to change the meetings you attend, you will have to challenge these beliefs and assumptions. There are far better ways to hold meetings. Meetings should not be "relaxation zones", but forums where the most difficult issues can be thrashed out. They should not be for the weak-hearted. And you can influence the effectiveness of meetings without being the chairperson.

WHAT KIND OF MEETINGS ARE THERE?

Before trying to improve the quality of the meetings in your business, you need to identify what kind of meetings you really need. There are many types of meeting. So your first job is to consider which is most suitable for your purpose, and if a meeting is even the best option.

A common complaint I hear when I ask employees about their meetings is that meetings get in the way of work. They interrupt the real work and create more work and prevent people doing any work. So, why have meetings at all?

The most common reason for calling a meeting is "sharing of information". These are the meetings where you all sit around, listening to updates from other attendees which have little relevance to you. You plough through spreadsheets, sleep-walk through slides and doodle through Any Other Business.

Sharing information is a very poor use of meeting time. Inevitably, if there are 10 people present, 90% of the meeting content will be irrelevant to you and the 10% which is about you, you already know. You are just repeating it for the benefit of other people who probably don't want to hear about it.

There is an argument that getting the team together for a round-up of information regularly is important (see Daily Check-In and Weekly Tactical below), but there are alternative mechanisms for communicating information. You can use email, intranet sites and even conversations face to face to pass information around. Over-reliance on your weekly meeting as the only source of information sharing wastes time and gives meetings a bad name.

However, another reason for holding a meeting is to consider a problem, generate possible solutions and make a decision.

Related to this are meetings held to learn from mistakes and successes. These are very good reasons to hold a meeting. You get everyone who has an interest, a perspective, expertise and influence, in to a room to thrash it out together. The idea of these meetings is to find the areas of conflict – What are the sticking points? What are the dangers? What are the risks? What are the different opinions? What are the potential gains? What can we learn?[2]

If you've never attended a really great meeting like this, let me illustrate how it might feel. In such meetings, everyone is entitled to a view. It doesn't matter whether that view reflects the views of anyone else in the meeting or whether it is purely personal. Everyone who has something to add is entitled to add it. Ultimately a decision will need to be taken and, if agreement cannot be made, the leader (or someone who has been given final veto) makes the call. Once the decision has been made, everyone in the team commits to abiding by that decision. The only reason to continue the debate is if new information comes to light.

I realize that most meetings aren't like this, and we'll see why below. But unless meetings are going to work along these lines there is very little reason to have them. The illusion of participation – where a meeting is called to "explore options" but where a decision has already been made, the leader is not open to persuasion, and politics and power-play rule over proper debate – is just as bad as a dictatorship. Worse, possibly, because in a dictatorship at least you know where you stand. When leaders try to convince us of their commitment to participation but are actually closed to ideas which contradict theirs, it is hard to know what behaviour is acceptable.

Separate operational issues from strategic issues

Most meetings are rather haphazard affairs. They happen because they always happen and they follow the same agenda format every time. Most executives say that they set meeting priorities based on the crisis of the moment, historical precedent or egalitarianism. They either lurch from urgent problem to urgent problem, or deal with HR policy because it is November, or assign equal time to each member's issue so that everyone gets a chance.

In addition, the agenda items are put in order based on a "first come, first served" basis – if you let the PA know your issue first, it will be first on the agenda. The person putting together the agenda often won't know how long a certain item requires, so roughly the same time boundary is assigned to all items. I am not blaming PAs here. The agenda may be put together by the team leader and he or she may also not know how significant a particular item is until everyone is sitting together in the meeting room.

Because of this, strategic issues rarely make it on to the agenda. It is only when it becomes urgent to talk strategy (because of a crisis or looming deadline) that it is given time. But strategic discussions are often long, drawn-out affairs (if you do them right), and fitting those conversations into a packed agenda of urgent operational issues means that we deal with them in the same way as we deal with a crisis. We don't do our research. We don't take time to fully consider the implications. We don't debate all the options. We make a snap decision which a minority disagree with and hope it won't come back to bite us.

Michael C. Mankins, co-author of *The Value Imperative: Managing for Superior Shareholder Returns* found that separating operational and strategic issues means far more time is spent on strategy without adding to the overall meetings burden. ABN AMRO split board meetings in two 10 years ago. Instead of meeting twice a week for 3 hours to discuss operations, it met only once a week to discuss operations and once a month, for a full day, to debate strategy and make decisions about how to allocate resources.[3]

As a result, the senior team actually ended up spending less time in meetings but far more of that time on strategic issues, moving from an average of 1 hour a month to about 10 hours a month.

Four meetings

In addition to separating operational issues and strategic issues, the remaining meetings should also be reorganized. Patrick Lencioni, the author of *Death by Meeting*, believes there are four types of meeting any organization needs:[4]

1. *Daily Check-In.* At some point every morning you and your colleagues should spend 5 minutes bringing each other up-to-date on your plans for the day. The purpose is to avoid confusion about who is doing what. These are not 90-minute meetings. They are not where people bring problems. They are not where people show off about how busy they are. It is not a competition. They simply require everyone to state what they are working on that day in order to minimize poor communication. When we can see how what we are doing is influenced by what everyone else is doing (and vice versa), potential conflicts of activity are avoided (e.g. Alan is leaving the office

to visit Bill 100 miles away on the same day that Charlie is meant to be having a 1-2-1 meeting with Alan).

2. *Weekly Tactical.* This meeting focuses on issues of immediate concern. Everyone on the team should attend and it should last 45–90 minutes. Any temptation to discuss strategy should be avoided. These meetings are operational and the facilitator should be robust around this. The purpose of this meeting is to review progress and agree next steps. It also helps everyone present focus on top priorities and not get distracted by projects which have personal interest but don't contribute to the success of the team or the organization. When you arrive you should each state what you are working on, and when you leave the meeting you should feel clear about what you are expected to do and how your progress is going to be measured. Each week, attendees will update their colleagues on their commitments from last week. This ensures the team is constantly moving forward and not using meetings to stall, point-score or take a nap.

    Any major issues which require brainstorming, analysis or preparation should be delayed until the next meeting – the monthly strategic.

3. *Monthly Strategic.* This is where difficult issues and problems are wrestled with by the team. Strategic meetings should be monthly, although additional ad hoc strategic meetings can be held if an urgent strategic issue arises. Remember though – strategic issues should not be handled in weekly tactical meetings even in an emergency. The tone and feel of the meetings should be kept separate, even if one occurs directly after the other with only a tea break and a chocolate biscuit in between.

The focus of the strategic meeting is to deep-dive into one or two topics which need more thought. Expect a strategic meeting to last about 2 hours *per issue*. In addition, you may need to do some preparation in advance in order that the meeting explores real data as well as the opinions around the room. If someone asks "How much did our competitors make out of introducing this idea 18 months ago?" it is useful if the information is available. Without it decisions made in such meetings don't stick because people doubt whether they were made correctly.

4. *Quarterly Off-Site Review.* Yes, quarterly. Not every 6 months. Not annually. This isn't about going golfing or playing mindless team-building games. The off-site is about reviewing the business in a more holistic and long-term manner. At off-sites I am involved in, the focus includes:

-   Direction setting – ensuring the company is headed in the right direction given economic and competitive realities.
-   "Elephants in the room" – delicate issues which have been rumbling under the surface but require time and space in a safe environment to be aired and resolved.
-   Personal issues – the individuals present share information about themselves in order to build trust and demonstrate transparency and honesty.
-   Personnel issues – the best and poorest performers in the business are discussed and plans are made for how to deal with them.
-   Creative thinking – time is set aside for considering the competition, changes in the market, learning from related

industries and even learning from unrelated industries in order to generate fresh ideas about how to grow the business.

Off-sites should always have some practical outcomes, but they should also provide ample time to mull over issues and consider options which lie outside the normal and everyday. Debating around a subject and providing time for personal anecdote and revelation adds depth to working relationships and often leads to an "ah-ha" moment, where the solutions to seemingly intractable problems suddenly emerge.

Having these four types of meeting has an added benefit. People always know where an issue or concern can be "parked". Currently, you may feel that if you don't raise a strategic issue at your weekly team meeting you won't be able to raise it at all. If you knew that the monthly strategic meeting was the place for such issues, you would ensure it was on the agenda and be able to focus on shorter-term issues in the meantime.

Reorganizing meetings may be within your remit. If it isn't, some ideas for influencing the content of meetings you attend are given later in this chapter. If it is, you can begin by reshuffling your meetings to fit one of these four basic meeting types. This may mean removing certain meetings from the diary, reorganizing the frequency of other meetings and changing the way agendas are used. You will want to communicate with the other attendees your reasons for shaking up these meetings, and ensure they are clear on the purpose of each meeting.

It is likely that people will test out the rigidity of the new meeting structure by trying to raise strategic issues in weekly meetings or discussing problems during the daily check-in. If you are flexible about these delineations, the attendees will learn not to trust this new structure and will revert back to old behaviours. Politely remind people of the structure and format of each meeting and never make exceptions. This includes ensuring you don't break the rules yourself. Be disciplined.

If your meetings don't seem to fall into any of these categories, you could ask yourself – does the meeting have any value? Spending 3 hours purely updating the chair of the meeting isn't a good use of anyone's time except, perhaps, the chair. Such updates could be done in one-to-one meetings or by speaking to colleagues informally on a more regular basis. Each member of the meeting doesn't need to sit through this level of detail on a weekly basis to do their job. If they do, there is a bigger issue to be resolved at the quarterly off-site – How do we improve communication on a daily basis so it doesn't take 45 minutes to understand what any one of my colleagues is working on?

WHAT SHOULD THE GROUND RULES OF MEETINGS BE?

Whenever I facilitate a meeting I start out with a ground rules exercise. It is important that the meeting attendees have agreed on acceptable and unacceptable behaviour and articulated the kinds of problem that get in the way of an effective use of time. When people feel they have contributed to these ground rules they have greater ownership. They tend to speak out if anyone disrespects those ground rules and they hold themselves to a higher standard because they openly stated at the start what they expect of others.

However, I have never seen this done at any of the meetings I have attended as a participant. Why should it be that ground rules are important when you bring in an outside facilitator but not for "internal" meetings?

One argument is that when an organization brings in an outside facilitator it is, by its nature, a more significant meeting. You wouldn't bother with a facilitator for a weekly tactical (would you?) and, because they happen so frequently, there is already an understanding of the ground rules. They don't need to be reviewed every time.

Except that this assumes there are unwritten ground rules – a code which all attendees hold themselves to without needing formal recognition – and that these informal ground rules create the right sort of tone for getting work done well. We all know that this is not true, that people behave in ways that inhibit participation, prevent honesty and encourage consensus rather than debate. That's why we see certain people dominating the meeting without being curtailed by the chair. That's why we see decisions being made that many attendees cannot get behind. That's why we see endless debate of insignificant matters while the real issue is avoided.

I would argue that ground rules create the environment and that, unless you transparently create them and then transparently review them, you will end up with an unwritten rulebook based on hierarchy, power and historical precedent.

Here are some common ground rules which have proven very helpful in the meetings I run:

1. *Confidentiality: What happens in the room stays in the room.* This ground rule shouldn't get in the way of communicating the meetings outcomes or even the arguments that were presented in the meeting. But it should ensure that private conversations in the meeting do not become the gossip of the business. Meetings can be a place where people express their vulnerabilities or even show emotion. People need to feel they can do this without any detriment to their status in the business at large. Discussing what confidentiality means is important. Assuming everyone has the same understanding is dangerous.

2. *Participation, to your own level of stretch.* People should not be required to take up equal airtime. Some people prefer to think before speaking. Others think as they speak. Some people will speak to confirm their agreement with a previous speaker. Others stay quiet if they have nothing original to add. Participation to your own level of stretch means that everyone challenges themselves to participate in ways that help them grow. Someone might speak more than usual as a way to stretch themselves. Someone else might speak less. However, by agreeing to this ground rule everyone acknowledges their responsibility to get involved.

3. *Cabinet responsibility.* This ground rule means that, once a decision has been taken, it is final and there is no further debate unless new evidence becomes available. This is important because whilst everyone should feel they can express their view honestly, once the decision is taken it must be implemented. If there is still informal debate, politicking and gossip because the final decision didn't please everyone, consistent action will not follow. As long as everyone feels they were able to express their opinion and that the decision was taken with these opinions in mind, everyone must present a united face when they begin communicating the decision to the rest of the organization.

4. *Attend meetings and be on time.* This hardly needs any explanation. However, meetings that don't start on time encourage lateness. Those who did arrive on time think "why should I waste my time waiting for everyone else?" and they start coming to meetings later in future. When people miss meetings they give others the impression that they don't respect their colleagues. Again, this is infectious and people start point-scoring, competing about who is most in demand and who has the busiest schedule. One meeting I attend has a firm rule – if you cannot attend you must demonstrate the clear business imperative for not being there and communicate this to all attendees *before* the meeting. Whilst people do miss the meeting on occasion, the message is clear – this meeting is important for business too.

5. *Listen and show respect for other people.* This means no interrupting, ridiculing, sidelining or attacking other people. One of the key purposes of a meeting is to draw out conflict

(more on this later). People cannot share conflicting opinions if they fear judgement. This doesn't mean you can't give feedback. It must be possible to stop someone dominating the meeting and sometimes this means stopping them while they talk. But the commitment around listening and showing respect helps everyone stand up for their right to participate.

6. *Phones off.* And laptops. And that includes the chair. A fine for breaking this rule normally works quite well. If the meeting is important, it requires your focus. If it isn't important, why are you there?

7. *One meeting.* Sidebar conversations are disruptive. They also imply that issues are not being shared with everyone, which is getting in the way of a good, solid decision. If you notice sidebar conversations, stop what you are doing and draw attention to what is going on.

8. *Work towards outcomes.* Depending on the type of meeting you are having, this ground rule has variable meaning. At a check-in meeting it means that you focus on what you are there to do – a 60-second-per-person update. At a quarterly off-site it means having the rigorous debate required to establish the company's direction. At a monthly and weekly meeting it means getting to a good decision so that action can commence. There should be a sense that all conversations have a purpose and, if they don't, that you have some means of moving on to a more fruitful subject.

9. *Ensure credit is given.* Meetings can be rufty-tufty affairs and they can move at quite a pace. One person sparks another person and that's how new ideas emerge. However, in the fray,

some people contribute without being credited. I am sure you have been in a meeting where you shared an idea which was duly ignored only to have a colleague repeat the same idea later to much acclaim! Simply saying "This idea came to me when Joe was speaking" is often enough credit for Joe to continue making a contribution in future. If you notice someone was not credited by another colleague you can say "Great idea James. And Joe, thanks for your part in that too" or the equivalent. Participation should be recognized.

10. *The only stupid question is the one that isn't asked.* One reason people don't participate is the fear of looking stupid. As a professional facilitator I can ask stupid questions because I am not expected to know everything. But, funnily enough, when I do I open the floodgates for lots of similar questions from other people in the meeting. It is as if I have given people permission to be stupid. Of course, there isn't such a thing as a stupid question. If you are thinking it, other people probably are too. And, even if they aren't, unless you ask it you will always wonder whether it should have been asked. The exception is where you haven't prepared for a meeting. If you have to ask a stupid question because you didn't read the pre-work, or didn't listen to a colleague's presentation, still ask your question. But don't make the same mistake next time.

How to create ground rules

It is far more powerful if the ground rules are created by the attendees than presented, fully formed, without discussion or debate.

Creating ground rules need not take long but can be a positive warm-up exercise, preparing people for what is coming next.

If I am helping a team to create meeting ground rules from scratch, I tend to ask attendees to make a list of what they don't want the meeting to be like before I ask them to make a list of what they do want the meeting to be like. On a flip chart I write in the "Don't want" column words and phrases generated by the group, like "Being interrupted", "Being ridiculed", "Gossip" and "No outcome". Then I ask what behaviour would ensure the meeting was very valuable and write this in the "Do want" column. If the ground rules above don't come up naturally, I make suggestions – although I only write them down if everyone agrees they should be ground rules. We often end up with about 20 words or phrases which reflect the ground rules the group wants to create.

If you have regular meetings and don't want to spend 10 minutes creating new ground rules each time, that is fine. But ensure the ground rules are displayed prominently, reviewed regularly and referred to during the meeting.

WHY DO CERTAIN PEOPLE DOMINATE AND OTHERS HOLD BACK?

There are many reasons why certain people take a greater or lesser part in a meeting. In some cases, it is just natural style. Some people are more introvert or extrovert and their level of participation doesn't tell you anything about whether the meeting is good or bad. You will know who is more outgoing and who is less outgoing in meetings (if you take the time to get to know people properly), and will not be overly concerned if certain individuals are less verbose than others.

The problem comes when some people actually dominate, getting in the way of an effective meeting or when other people hold back, getting in the way of an effective meeting.

Hobbyhorses and windbags. Some people like a stage and, especially if they feel they aren't generally given enough airtime, may dominate proceedings with their war stories or repetitive arguments. As John Barnes puts it:

> "Meetings are an opportunity to speak about things to a lot of people. They are an opportunity for some people to 'broadcast'. And that's to be avoided in my view. Broadcasting is of no value. What you want is interaction."

In such cases it is acceptable to interrupt. Something like, "This is familiar turf. Does anyone have something new to add?" may reopen the floor to others who haven't yet spoken. Alternatively, a private word with the individual or a question in private, such as

"When we get on to this topic you seem to get stuck on one issue. What's causing this?" can help you draw attention to the problem, understand it more clearly and help the individual concerned to move on too.

Speaking in order to encourage participation. Some people speak up because they think, by doing so, they are modelling the kind of participation they want to see from others. It is a common technique by leaders who want to encourage openness. They will ask a question and when no one responds they say, "Well, in that case, let me start". They then share their view, hoping to set the tone but actually obstructing anyone else from speaking. No one wants to be first to disagree with the boss. Plus, the boss always rescues everyone and lets them off the hook. So next time the boss asks a similar question, the other attendees wait for him or her to answer it without anyone else's contribution. The leader's positive intention actually gets in the way of participation.

Instead, if you ask a question, sit with the silence. Eventually someone will speak. It doesn't always have to be you.

Disenfranchisement or resentment. Sometimes people withhold their participation as a form of protest. They may believe there is something false about the request for participation and that taking part is a waste of time. They may think that they can postpone decision-making or delay change if they withhold their participation and, if they are afraid of change or disagree with planned changes, slowing the whole process down can be in their interest. They may be testing the leader – has she noticed they haven't yet spoken? Has he taken the loud-mouths in hand?

Whatever the reason, it is possible to draw these people out. One way is by demonstrating that participation has value, that you are genuine when you ask for ideas and that ill-formed ideas or contrary opinions won't be judged.

Another way is to ask them privately for their views on the meeting and how the meeting could be more valuable for them. It may take time for them to trust you, but it is worth it if you believe they have value to add. If you don't, what are they doing there?

Shy or unconfident. Of course, sometimes people want to speak but it is a huge challenge for them. They may believe there are unwritten rules relating to seniority and, if they are relatively junior, they may believe it is simply good etiquette to withhold their opinion. They may believe their views are unimportant or even stupid. Such people often have great ideas and a huge amount to add but the structure of the meeting makes that difficult.

In addition to some one-to-one conversations to see if you can coach them to be more confident, you can look at how to reorganize the meeting to make it easier for them to take part.

One option is to break the group into small subgroups to discuss certain issues, which then report back to the larger group, workshop style. This is unusual in a meeting and far more common on a training course. But the reason trainers break people into small groups is that it makes it easier for some people to log their viewpoint. A more outgoing person can then represent the opinions of their small group to the larger group and all opinions are heard.

Another option is to encourage debate before the meeting via an intranet forum or just by email. Some people prefer to submit their opinion in writing. Once they have done that they sometimes feel more confident speaking too. With a little encouragement they may repeat what they wrote, but in more depth.

Use any material available to elicit ideas and opinions. Post-It notes work a treat. Ask attendees to write their ideas or their questions or concerns on Post-Its and stick these on a wall or on a chart created for this purpose. Depending on the subject under discussion, you will get an idea of who is against and who is for, what the concerns and questions are, and whether any themes emerge.

This helps those who tend to hold back. But it also helps those who tend to dominate. It breaks the patterns that tend to evolve in meetings and, by changing the meeting style, you wrong-foot people who use meetings for their own ends. Their usual behaviour doesn't work. So they give up and get stuck in to the matter at hand.

Emotions. Strong emotions can prevent people from participating fully and get in the way of them presenting their ideas well. However, I have nothing against emotion in meetings. In fact, I think there is too little emotion in meetings. We just need to handle it properly. We don't want people leaving the room crying because they were ignored, blamed or ridiculed. However, when people feel strongly (as we hope they will) about their work and their ideas, we want to know.

I have seen leaders powerfully use their own emotions to encourage participation. One leader I work with speaks about feeling disappointed, moved, hurt and even loved in his meetings. By sharing his emotions so openly he encourages other people to express theirs.

By asking people how they "feel" as well as what they "think" we are able to understand the problem which needs to be resolved more clearly. For instance, if one of your sales team members feels disappointed by last month's sales figures, you can ask – "What results would prevent you feeling disappointed next time?" and discover what targets he believes are more appropriate.

Rather than seeing emotions as a problem, explore how they can be demonstrated more transparently and how they can contribute to the robustness of decisions.

MISSING MEETINGS

Many of the people I interviewed had stopped going to meetings that were a waste of time. And yet when I mention this option to clients who complain about the meetings in their organization, they balk at the suggestion. One reason is that they have a rather low opinion of colleagues who do the same. When a colleague misses a meeting they can become the subject of gossip. They are seen as breaking ranks, showing disrespect or being superior. Some people would rather attend a bad meeting than be seen as an outsider, so they continue to go to these meetings, complain about the non-attendance of others and avoid the real issue – why is this meeting so bad that people don't want to be here?

Whilst one of my ground rules is to attend all meetings and be on time, I know that people will miss meetings if they feel they have no value. If a meeting is plagued by non-attendance, either by the same people time and time again, or by different people at different times for a wide range of reasons, you have to ask yourself whether they are really dealing with something urgent and important or whether, quite frankly, anything is more urgent and important than this meeting. Getting strict about the ground rules won't help you much if the meeting is truly a waste of time. A review of the scope, purpose and value of the meeting is then in order. And if you are guilty of non-attendance because the meeting is a bad one but you haven't actually tried to address the underlying problem, then you haven't really acted like a leader. A leader (or a good manager) would have addressed the problem before taking the coward's way out – avoiding any confrontation and keeping their opinions to themselves.

But there is a valid reason to miss meetings and that is when you aren't needed. People get invited to meetings for a variety of reasons. You may be invited out of historical precedent. You may be invited because of your influence. You may be invited because the meeting is seen as a good alternative to communicating face to face, one to one. You may be invited because you are the boss and the team doesn't feel valued if you aren't there. You may be invited because you are the boss and the team wants you to see how hard it works. I could go on.

You will have to judge why you have been invited and therefore how to handle the prospect of not attending in future. If your team feels under-valued, there may be other ways to reassure them which don't require 3 hours every Thursday. If you are invited because of your influence, you may want to help your colleagues develop influence of their own. Consider the possible reasons behind your invitation to attend a meeting (or ask directly why you are needed) and, where possible, resolve the underlying issue rather than just accepting that your colleagues feel you are indispensable.

It doesn't have to be disruptive to end your attendance at meetings. Belinda is a middle manager in the NHS, who took matters into her own hands:

"I am probably quite good at wheedling my way out of meetings if I don't need to be there. I literally go to my manager and say I don't have anything to contribute to that and I am not sure why I am needed. Some people resign themselves to the pointlessness of things but I question everything. Influence the agenda or chair it

Continued

yourself so you get what you need from it, but if you really feel you have nothing to contribute argue that case with your manager. There are often very clear reasons why you don't need to be there. Obviously you've got to try to input. It isn't acceptable to sit there, not making an effort. But part of being a line manager is to listen to questions and if they are valid to act accordingly. I've never had any bad fall out from that."

Karen Mellor says that simply asking the right question can help the chair of the meeting to clarify its purpose and spark a review:

"If you are relatively junior you just have to ask the question 'Could you share some objectives with me because I am finding it difficult to see where my contribution may lie?' You could either do that in the meeting or offline."

It seems that questioning your attendance at meetings can actually be good for your career. As long as your intention is to add value, to do the best job you can and to achieve your objectives, you are unlikely to be seen as a trouble-maker.

THE POLITICS OF MEETINGS

The meeting isn't really the meeting. What I mean is that the formal meeting where you sit around the board table discussing the issues at hand is only part of the decision-making process. If you are wondering why your comments seem to be ignored, or why other people seem to have greater influence than you, it may be because you are putting too much faith in the meeting itself.

Getting involved in what happens before and after a meeting will help you ensure your viewpoint or issue is given due importance. Karen Mellor is in charge of setting the agendas for her team. She explains the process she has developed:

> "We have 12 members based all over the world and we have 4 face-to-face meetings a year where we get together for 3 or 4 days. That's where we agree our goals, mission and project areas and we have a 2-hour conference call once a month to deal with operational issues. Everyone can put in agenda items and they have to say how long they want and what they want to walk away with. The meeting is then run to the time unless we get into a really rich topic and then we will go over but we 'timebox' it. If we go over that timebox we agree another time to carry on. We have 'pods' where we identify 4 people to work it out offline and that's what happens to those items."

Karen's process shows that the work of the meeting starts well before the PowerPoint projector is fired up. Members of the team contribute to the agendas in advance and consider what they want to walk away with as a result. They don't just say "I want us to talk about the office heating system", they say "I want 32 minutes to discuss the office heating system and I want to walk away with a decision on whether we should replace the boiler this year or review in 12 months".

You can see that a clear focus on outcomes is far more likely to result in a decision. It may not be the decision you wanted, but it will be a decision nonetheless. At least you will know where you stand. The issue does not need to be discussed again for 12 months (or at such time as the boiler decides to give up the ghost).

Paul Currah, a procurement manager, goes a step further. He realized after a number of years in business the importance of influencing opinions at every opportunity, not waiting for the meeting to resolve issues:

"The informal stuff of work achieves as much as the formal stuff of work. I started my career thinking there were formal ways of getting stuff on a meeting agenda or persuading people of a particular course of action. But a lot of what gets done gets done outside the meeting. And a lot of the influencing needs to happen before, during and after a meeting. It is not just about relying on your 5-minute slot in a meeting to persuade everyone that what you are proposing is the right thing to do. If you are able to get people used to the idea before the meeting and provide a compelling argument in the meeting and follow up afterwards to ensure those people have made the right decision, then that is the most powerful way to get things done. That informal part of

Continued

going to see people, having corridor conversations, sowing seeds, chatting with people offline, selling to different constituents the same thing but packaged differently, all that informal persuasion and influencing, that's 90% of a decision."

"What happens in the meetings, that's only 10%."

Some people feel uncomfortable with this approach, labelling it as politics and therefore "bad". As I wrote in my last book, *The Recipe for Success*, there is nothing innately bad about politics. What matters is where your motivation comes from.[5] I would not advocate personal power battles where you manipulate opinions in order to scupper the promotion chances of your sworn enemy, or backstabbing in order to make your colleagues look like fools. But, to be honest, this kind of politics is rare. What you are really seeing when you observe politics, is managers who believe in a cause, believe it is right for the business, right for their people and, probably, right for themselves. They then use their emotional intelligence to communicate with different populations in order to explain their beliefs and, hopefully, persuade others of their validity. By the time the meeting happens, some important conversations have already happened.

Ian Hill is a middle manager who has worked all over the world. He has walked this thin but important line, learning to become more skilled throughout his career:

"When I worked in Italy the culture was that when a matter was coming up in a meeting you met up with people for lunch beforehand, you talked, made your alliances, got to the meeting and your way carried the day. But it was more persuasion than manipulation. I have sometimes come away from meetings where I felt things were manipulated. I have influenced meetings. I have unintentionally dominated meetings."

"That's been part of my learning and development as a manager. If you are a strong character like a lot of managers it is hard not to dominate and hard not to make your way carry the day. But you are not going to be right 100% and you are missing a richness of intellect that can improve what you are doing. A lot of decisions have unintended consequences beyond our thought horizon. You can make some decisions in a meeting and you have thought things through as well as you can but you don't have time to think through every step and you miss the last one sometimes. Down the line you realize there is a problem and you explore what's really gone wrong and you find it goes back to something you persuaded people to do 6 months ago and you hadn't seen that consequence."

What Ian is highlighting is that, whilst the influencing before, during and after the meeting is important, it must be a two-way process. If you are going to influence, you also need to be open to influence. The meeting isn't the only place where you will influence minds. But equally, other people will want to influence you between meetings too. Recognizing this means you will set aside time for those informal conversations. This has multiple benefits.

You will know the various arguments around this issue which will help you be more persuasive. You will know the various arguments around the issue which will help you see flaws in your position. You will be able to see where ideas are coming from so you can give credit where it is due. You will be able to form bonds with colleagues because you have spent time with them informally. You will be able to learn more about the business than you could simply by listening to presentations in a meeting. You will have time to think of win/win solutions rather than being surprised by a contrary solution in the meetings and having no time to consider its implications.

And, ultimately, you will all make better-informed, more robust, more innovative decisions in the meeting because you have had time to discuss, digest, brainstorm and understand over a period of weeks and not just 90 minutes around a table.

HOW TO MAKE A DECISION

Of course, you must also set aside time and create a mechanism for making decisions in the meeting. Without a decision, a meeting is a waste of time. The decision may not be made quickly, in the moment, but all discussions and debates should be heading towards the decision-making phase.

Let's say your team has been discussing an issue for the last 90 minutes and has generated 12 top-quality ideas. How do you decide which idea to go for and make a decision that sticks?

There are various steps to take when making decisions:

1. Identify the success criteria for a good idea before you select or deselect ideas. You may decide that a successful idea has to be cheap, popular and quick to implement. Or you may decide the successful idea has to be innovative, increase profit margins by at least 5% and be ready to implement within 2 years. Deciding these success criteria can be done in a meeting. Encourage debate, conflict and honesty in considering the most suitable success criteria for the project. Then generate ideas freely, without limits. Then, finally, reject any ideas which don't meet these criteria.

2. Of those ideas left in the frame, either vote or let the leader decide. Whilst voting has obvious advantages, a final decision by the leader, having taken all the arguments into account, usually sticks better. People are less likely to feel that a poor decision was made or that they were outvoted based on personality or popularity.

3. Separate debate from decision-making. Sometimes debate is quickly followed by the need to decide. However, sometimes

time is needed between the debate and the final decision. Perhaps more research is required. Perhaps people need time to digest all the arguments they have heard. Or perhaps the leader needs to decide how to communicate his or her final decision. Even if there is a full week between the debate and a decision (leaving you frustrated by the slow pace and hanging on tenterhooks), this is likely to be a more efficient system of decision-making than you have now.

4. Even bad ideas which do not meet the success criteria should be captured and stored. A bad idea today may turn out to be a good idea next year. A bad idea for this situation may be a great idea for the next similar but different situation. By storing the ideas your people come up with you demonstrate that you value their contribution. Revisit old ideas occasionally as a way to spark your imagination or fast-track the brainstorming process in future. It is a shame to lose those ideas and have to start afresh every time you meet.

WHAT CAN YOU DO WHEN YOU DON'T RUN THE MEETING?

If the meetings you attend are not run by you, it is time to start taking more responsibility. When I work with teams of middle managers I often hear the complaint that "they" don't listen, "they" will never change and "they" don't seem to care about the business or the people that work in the business. "They" is senior management.

If a meeting really is a waste of time, non-attendance is often an option. But what everyone I spoke to felt, was that you have more influence than you think. Your manager wants results from you. Good results from you reflect well on him or her. If you can demonstrate how your results are being hindered by a meeting *and* what you would be able to achieve if the meeting was redesigned, there is very little case against. Tread gently, because any criticism of the meeting may be perceived as a criticism of the leader who chairs it. But this doesn't mean you must avoid the issue.

If you don't have enough influence as an individual, you may want to recruit some supporters. An analysis of the outcomes of the previous meetings may be persuasive. If countless meetings have resulted in little decisive action, there is an argument that any change would certainly not be worse than the status quo.

If a wholesale meetings review is too extreme, it may be worth changing just one or two of the worst meetings. Keep a record of the changes you have made and note any difference in outcomes. If there is ever a temptation to revert to old ways, you will have some pretty impressive data.

Paul Currah has realized, during his career in management, that we often perceive ourselves to have little influence:

"The reality is that most of us have more influence than we think. If I am not having influence I wonder if I am not performing well enough, if I am not having the right conversations or I'm not using the right language or making the most of my opportunities and therefore I need to improve those influencing skills to make myself more effective."

Instead of accepting that lack of influence is a fact of life, see what opportunities you have to gain great influence. Ask yourself what stops you taking action over and above the accepted norms of someone in your role. Do you genuinely have a legitimate fear, or are your concerns more about "form"?

Middle manager Belinda has challenged herself about this and believes fear of what other people think often lies at the root of a perceived lack of influence:

"People worry about what other people think of them at work all the time. If I was them I would worry about being good at their job. Work can be like the school playground. But if you can just focus on doing your job well and stop focusing on plotting you'd be able to do a good job and give clear directions and help others see how your job is important. And that keeps me well enough occupied. It can feel like an arena but doing your job well pays off."

MEETINGS – FINAL THOUGHTS

It is not possible to run an organization single-handed. It requires other people. But as soon as you get two people working together you start getting meetings. Before long, your time is dominated by meetings with peers, direct reports, customers and clients, potential customers and clients, your manager, shareholders, the local community, charitable foundations, mentors, former colleagues, troublesome colleagues … Even lunch with a friend has to be scheduled like a meeting.

Because meetings are such a dominant part of our working lives they provide a great opportunity to get a big bang for your buck. Start making inroads into the way meetings are structured, facilitated and focused on results and you start seeing the impact during and outside the meeting.

Remember what the prize is – a dramatic reduction in wasted time and the capitalization of the talent in the room. Just by changing one meeting you start to cut wasted time and access more of what you and your colleagues have to offer. Multiply that by all the meetings you attend and the results can transform your company.

Meetings also provide you with an opportunity to try flexing those manager muscles. Even a small change can make a big difference to your working life, so taking a few risks, experimenting with how far your influence stretches, trying a different style of communication with your manager, shaking up the process to see if people will change their habits … all of this gives you the confidence to try something bigger and more dramatic later. Changing meetings is a good test-bed for skills and approaches you might use later to challenge more fundamental problems in the business.

You may not see much success the first time you try. But rather than giving up and thinking "nothing will ever change in this place", ask yourself what you could do differently next time. What was it about your efforts which meant your suggestions landed on stony ground? How can you have another go and get a different result?

That's what great managers (and great leaders) do all the time. They ask difficult questions, they bring about change, they look at how to get the best from the people around them. Does this sound like your line manager? Or is he someone who just seems to shuffle paper, give orders and hide in his office all day? Let's look at the next great Frustration of work – leadership.

Frustration 2: Mis-Leadership

It was the third product recall in as many weeks. The first time, Larry had been enthusiastic about communicating the company line to his customers, confident that the recall was happening for all the right reasons. A flaw in one component had been noticed and although there was no proof the product would malfunction, the company was doing its due diligence and asking all its customers – large high-street stores and out-of-town "sheds" – to remove the items from their shelves and return them to the supplier for a full refund.

In fact, Larry felt even more loyal to his employer because it seemed to be taking its relationship with customers so seriously.

The second time it happened he felt less positive. Having just told customers there would not be any more recalls and that the first was just evidence of the company's high standards, he had to go back to them again about a different product and repeat the same message. He felt that trust between himself and the customer was being tested and it was just as well he had built such strong relationships over the last five years. What annoyed him just a little was that the story had been broken not by his senior manager but by the press. Customers were already ringing him on the phone before he was ready with a message to give them. And, instead of his boss calling the sales team together to explain the latest product flaw and work with them to agree a strategy for keeping customers satisfied, he had reacted late and with an email which just told them "Keep telling them what you told them last time".

The third recall had Larry ready to hand in his resignation. Like his colleagues, all junior sales managers like himself, he had received no thanks from his senior sales manager boss or anyone else in the company for the difficult job they had been doing over the last two weeks. They had barely seen each other, except when his boss scurried past him, head in a pile of papers, passing from one high-level meeting to another. As he was without a lot of the information he required, Larry could not reassure his own team of salespeople about whether the third recall would be the last and what the strategy for rebuilding relationships with customers was going to be.

Larry had gone from thinking of his manager as a father figure who cared about his team and respected the customer to a distant relative who had no idea about what it was like on the coal face.

By the time we met for our one-to-one coaching session, Larry was ready to snap.

The most common reason I get asked to work with companies today is "leadership development". There is a recognition that, if they are going to give people the title "leader" or "manager", they had better know what that means and be able to live up to that standard.

However, many organizations are rather unclear about what a leader is supposed to do and even more unclear about the difference between a leader and a manager, if there is one. It often feels that, when we look at our own managers, we learn more about what *not* to do than about what *to* do. And if the organization (by which I mean the people at the very top who create the culture) is unsure about what management and leadership should look like, how on earth are you supposed to know?

I am going to outline some different ways to view leadership and management and start to identify some key characteristics and beliefs of top leaders and managers. I will look at what annoys people so much about managers and leaders (and what you can do to manage your manager better) and why people find leadership and management so difficult to do (and how you can be a better manager yourself).

However, you will need to decide what kind of manager or leader you want to be. No one can tell you how to do it "right". The days of black and white, right and wrong, good and bad, are gone (if they ever really existed). The world and the workplace are ever-changing. What worked yesterday won't work today. Everything you thought you knew is just speculation and assumption. It is possible that by the end of this chapter you will be even more confused about what your job really is.

But don't worry. As one of my mentors, the natural horsemanship expert David Harris puts it, "Confusion is good. It means you know there are lots of options out there. If you're not confused, you are probably just ignorant".

WHAT IS LEADERSHIP? AND WHAT IS MANAGEMENT?

This is the biggie. Let's start by looking at what a couple of the academics say.

Marcus Buckingham, the author of *First, Break all the Rules*[1] and the man behind the Gallup Q12 survey defines managers and leaders as different animals:

> "Managers discover what is unique about each person and capitalize on it … Great managers know and value the unique abilities and even the eccentricities of their employees and they learn how best to integrate them in to a coordinated plan of attack. This is the exact opposite of what great leaders do. Great leaders discover what is universal and capitalize on it. Their job is to rally people towards a better future."[2]

Whilst he says one person can do both, that person must recognize the very different skills required.

Abraham Zaleznik, leadership expert at Harvard Business School, says managers seek order, control and rapid resolution of problems. They deal with the world as it is, working within the constraints they find around them. They are people-people but they try not to get too emotional. They prefer to reduce options and reduce risk. They don't like a lot of loose ends. And they are more interested in "how" than "what". For example, "How are we going to implement this policy?" versus "What policy shall we implement?"

Leaders, by contrast, are more like artists than scientists. They can tolerate chaos and lack of structure. They "shape" rather than respond to ideas. They relate to people empathetically and change how people think. They develop fresh approaches and direction and are often associated with strong emotions such as "love" and "hate".[3]

Whilst Zaleznik argues that organizations need managers *and* leaders, he believes that organizations are particularly bad at creating the environment where great leaders can thrive. By their nature, organizations are better at producing great managers.

Actually, I think the reality is that organizations are better at producing poor managers and poor leaders than great managers and great leaders, but I will explore why later on.

Speaking more from personal experience, John Barnes believes that management and leadership are not two distinct animals but two parts of the same person. This is how he describes the differences:

"When you start in management you have a large element of management to learn and a small element of leadership to learn. You become better as a manager so the amount of learning you have to do falls over time and you replace that with learning about leadership. If you are expert at being a manager you should be bouncing the ball on management. The leadership stuff should take more time because you aren't as expert at that. I think we are all both – managers and leaders."

John's argument is that, at any one time, you have some jobs which require a "manager's head" – the bit of you that needs to bring structure, order and certainty to complex problems – and some jobs which require a "leader's head" – the bit of you that needs to forge a direction, sit with complexity and solve problems creatively. At the start of your career you are on a steep learning curve in relation to your management abilities, so that predominates. As you progress up the hierarchy you still need all that management skill but it comes more naturally, so you can turn your thoughts to leadership.

He adds:

"Those people who say I am a leader so I only have to do leadership probably aren't very good at management, and therefore they probably aren't very good at leadership as well. It's very convenient for poor managers to say 'It doesn't matter because I only need to be a leader'. At the same time even your first line supervisor has a leadership responsibility. He is there to set the standards for the future, to inspire people to do things better, give them hope in a difficult situation. That's a part of their role on a daily basis with individuals who are probably more prepared to resist than higher up the organization."

This is why I am on something of a mission to reclaim "management" as a legitimate title. Leadership isn't better, it is just different. At all times you are being asked to flex between different management and leadership styles, adapting to the circumstances you find yourself in, the people you are working with and the particular problem you are trying to resolve.

Karen Mellor has held a variety of management and leadership positions throughout her career. She explains how she combines management and leadership in one role:

"You can do both – management and leadership. I have a global team across different sites and I have to manage to ensure we deliver, and I have to manage their careers. That's all management. But also I have a change agenda – how can we help this organization get the facts, make decisions quicker, make their lives easier. I think that part of it is more leadership. And you need leadership in every role even if you are just a team player in a group activity. You'd be able to mobilize projects faster, get people moving faster. If you are a manager and you can sell a concept with passion you are displaying leadership qualities. In order to get the respect of the people you are managing they need to look up to you as an inspirational leader."

That isn't to say you will find all aspects of this job come naturally to you. We all have different personalities, different preferences about how to behave at work and outside. Paul Currah says the journey towards becoming an exceptional leader and manager always presents challenges:

"I suspect some people are more naturally attuned to being a leader and others are more attuned to being a manager. I am by nature more attuned to being a manager but really enjoy being a leader too: most 'management' responsibilities require both roles to be performed. Where I have felt leadership is required I have put myself in to a position that says 'If this were my company or this part of the organization was mine to run, what would I want the people around me to engage with so that they can follow?' When I am in the manager frame of mind I am thinking 'How do we organize to get this done? What are the tactics that mean we can achieve what we are setting out to achieve?' The leader role is determining strategy and direction and the manager is about how we are going to realize that vision."

And, as well as manager and leader, you also have other responsibilities which could be labelled too. You could, at times, be most accurately described as a teacher. At other times you are a coach. Then, occasionally, you might be a guide or a strategist, a facilitator or a lobbyist, or even a parent. As we explore what your job actually is, I will aim to use the most appropriate word but usually I will just refer to leader-managers, meaning everything you are expected to be if you wish to excel. And if you want to grow you'll need to identify which aspects I describe as important are innate to you, which are strengths, which are a struggle and which you never even considered fall into your remit.

In the end, you will put together your own definition of your role and that will be unique to you. And it is in that way that you add value to your organization. Companies don't need "cookie cutter" managers coming off a production line who think alike and talk alike. Whether they realize it or not they need individuals who bring everything they have to offer to their workplace.

WHY ARE THERE SO FEW GREAT LEADER-MANAGERS?

In attempting to grow as a leader-manager you may find yourself rather isolated. If you are lucky, there is a culture in your organization of developing strong leader-managers. You will have role models you can look up to; you may have a mentorship scheme which connects you with impressive individuals inside or outside your company. You may be sent to seminars and lectures on the subject and your performance review may focus as much on these skills as your ability to reach financial targets.

If you are lucky.

If not, you are like most people. You've had some great bosses and some poor ones. You look around and see few people you would want to emulate. You want to be stretched but find your own line management struggling with the very same issues as you. You think "If they can't do this, or if they managed to get promoted without having to, why should I?"

This is where you'll need a bit of that leadership mindset. Leadership is about breaking rules, redefining the reality, thinking beyond the here and now. No matter how junior you are, you have the ability to imagine how the leadership culture in your organization can be different. If you can imagine it, you can start to "be" it. Ghandi said, "Be the change you want to see in the world". Here is your opportunity to be the change you want to see in your company.

But what are the obstacles you will encounter and why do they exist?

Organizations are complex systems. When the notion of the modern organization was dreamt up, it was based on the new science of the time, the science of the machine. Every aspect of a business was seen as part of a machine. If one part breaks, you fix it. If one part is broken beyond repair, you replace it. The assumption is that, if you get all of this right, the machine will tick over without trouble. What you need in such an environment is mechanics who can tend to the machine and carry out the necessary repairs. Of course, people do not behave like machines. They are unpredictable. They have bad days. They want to feel valued. They are responsible for the dreaded "human error".

In such a culture, people are seen as a problem. If only we could control people the same way that we control a machine (or do away with the people and just deal with machines), we could have a really efficient system which ran smoothly every day. Given that we cannot do away with people altogether, a manager's role in such an environment is to control and direct activity as precisely as possible. Unpredictability and change are to be avoided.

In a company run along these lines, most people with line responsibility are expected to demonstrate a command and control style of leadership. They may teach but they do this by demonstrating how they want a thing done and then expecting their direct reports to do it the same way. They may be interested in an employee's life outside of work, but only in so far as it affects performance.

This approach is very old-fashioned, but its legacy lingers. I've certainly heard clients exclaim how much they would enjoy work if it wasn't for the people. And I have heard employees described as cannon fodder, drones and the masses. Whilst all of this may have been in jest, I think it reveals some latent beliefs.

The new science is all about Quantum Theory.[4] This theory looks to nature for clues about the workings of the world. Business in this light is less like a machine and more like nature. An example is chaos theory – a butterfly beats its wings in London and someone gets promoted in New York. There is interconnectedness between different parts of the organization and the outside world. A shift in one part of the organization is felt elsewhere in the organization. Replacing a "broken part" in the sales department has a knock-on effect on morale in R&D.

In a more complex world it is impossible to manage all the detail of all the possible outcomes of any course of action. Command and control simply doesn't work because it assumes direct cause and effect, which can be predicted and contained. The reality is that an action today can have any number of predictable and unpredictable consequences and we cannot have a plan which covers every eventuality.

Managers and leaders in this kind of environment need to be adaptable. They need to sit with the discomfort of not knowing everything and not being able to control everything. They need to trust that, at each stage, they and the people around them will be able to resolve challenges. In this scenario people are not the problem, but the solution. The challenge is too complex to be solved by a machine. It must be solved in a more messy fashion where conflict, disagreement, emotion, humour, innovation, failure and risk-taking are all acceptable.

It's a perspective Jane Ginnever, Head of HR for a property management company, believes in strongly:

"I would like leaders to see their job as leading through people. People are the key asset. We all work and we are all looking for something out of our work, job satisfaction. We don't just go to work to get the pay packet, we want to be able to make a difference and work can change people's lives. If we can create companies which have people in them feeling they can make a difference and that they are valued, at all levels in the company, and that they know where they are going, that would be fantastic."

Although authors like Margaret Wheatley and Peter Senge have been writing about these principles for more than 20 years, it is still challenging stuff to senior managers who were rising through the ranks in the 1980s. When you look above you and wonder why few of your managers seem to know about these principles, remember that they were mentored by managers from a different age.

Expectations of work are increasing. As mentioned earlier, our expectations of work have changed. Since the 1960s, when the baby boomers started entering the workforce, work has become, for many people, more than just a job. (Some people clearly do it to pick up a pay packet at the end of the week, but they probably aren't reading this book. And if you are one of those people, it has probably become just a job to you because your expectations have been dashed. You didn't start out that way.) But the demands today's young recruits are making would have seemed just a dream to their grandparents.

Today, people want their work to have meaning. They want some flexibility around their hours. They want their organization to have a social responsibility. They want to feel valued. They want to see what part they play in the overall success of the business. 86% of Generation Y's (born late 1970s–2000) say it is important that their work makes a positive impact on the world. For them, high-quality colleagues, flexible working arrangements, recognition from their boss and access to new experiences and challenges are as important as – or more important than – financial rewards.

These rising expectations can be difficult for older leader-managers to handle. Leader-managers from Generation X (born 1961–1981) now hold positions in middle and senior management and know how hard it was for them to rise up the ranks. They know how many battles they fought and won just to get ergonomic chairs introduced and a veggie option in the staff cafeteria. They were the first generation to realize there was no such thing as a job for life. Increasingly, Generation X leader-managers are having to oversee juniors whom they are fundamentally out of step with. At the same time, we still have workers in the workforce who belong to the baby-boomer generation and refuse to retire. Three generations with increasingly high expectations all existing within one organization is bound to add complexity to the job of managing people.

However, this creates an opportunity for people like you who want to make their mark. As Sylvia Ann Hewlett, the founding president of the Center for Work–Life Policy in New York, puts it:

"The transformation of the workforce [managers] are now experiencing is a particularly dramatic one but hardly the last. The organizations that thrive will be those that recognize their people's shifting values and preferences – and that find ways to make the work meaningful on those terms."[5]

Leadership and management are hard to quantify. Organizations know the value of measuring performance. It is vital to know what your targets are and whether you are reaching them. Most targets are easily measurable, and so it is plain to see whether someone has achieved theirs or not. It is also relatively easy to measure certain aspects of "how" the job gets done. A company can work out that it takes, on average, 9 meetings to achieve a sale. Therefore, it may measure the numbers of meetings its sales people are having. A company can work out that customers like it if you answer the phone within three rings, so it measures how quickly you answer your phone. A company sees that highly engaged workers tend to arrive on time or early, so it monitors what time people are arriving as a way to judge who is engaged and who is not. These may not be great measures of performance (after all, it may take one person 11 meetings to make a sale worth £5m and someone else 5 meetings to make a sale worth only £100,000, so measuring the speed with which a sale is concluded isn't always meaningful), but they are simple and, combined, provide a useful picture of activity.

However, it is very difficult to measure management and leadership. Look again at what a great leader-manager does. Coaching, teaching, guiding, mentoring, parenting, visioning, strategising, organizing ... How can you tell whether an individual is good at this or not? You may say that you can measure the results in terms of team performance, staff turnover and how much the manager is liked and respected. However, this is complex because an employee might really like their manager because he gives them an easy time. Team performance may be great because the team got lucky with a good contract rather than because of the leadership they receive. A team may have a bad quarter because the manager has decided to focus on strategy rather than delivery and has made a calculation that short-term pain will be worth the long-term gain.

What this means is that managers, and the managers of managers, have few quantifiable clues about how well they are performing. They may have a sense that they are doing well but cannot easily discover whether they are deluding themselves or whether their instincts are accurate. I might rate your style of leadership because I recognize it as similar to my own. However, my own style of leadership may be flawed. I may respect your style of leadership because you are able to do things I cannot. However, I may be overly hard on myself and easy on you.

Because great leader-managers are hard to measure in terms of their behaviour, they find it hard to know what they should be doing. When their boss says "I want to see more leadership", neither party may have a clear view of what that means.

As Paul Currah pointed out earlier in this chapter, we all have certain styles of working which are more comfortable for us. Some people have a talent for organizing and they make this their focus. Picking up the phone to senior colleagues or holding one-to-one feedback sessions with direct reports feels less comfortable, so they avoid it.

They may not do this knowingly. In fact, they may have a perfectly good justification for why their style works best. Marshall Goldsmith, the author of *What Got You Here Won't Get You There*, says that many successful people reverse engineer their success and conclude that everything they do and everything they are must be responsible for their fast-track career.

However, whilst successful individuals are often successful *because* of what they do, they may also be successful *despite* what they do and often they don't know the difference.[6]

This is problematic. Firstly, it means that if you attempt to emulate them you will be repeating the same mistakes that they make. Secondly, it means they can't guide you because they have not accurately analysed the secret of their success.

When a whole senior team does this they create a dysfunctional culture in the organization, where poor leadership behaviours are perpetuated. In one company I work with (one of the biggest brands in the world), there is an acceptance that you can have your laptop open and work on emails during meetings. This is because that behaviour is demonstrated by the organization's top people. Perhaps (and this is speculation) employees think that they are demonstrating how intelligent they are because they can listen and write emails simultaneously. Maybe they are showing how important they are because they cannot walk away from their laptop for an hour. Maybe they are trying to communicate a not-too-subtle message to the meeting chair about the quality of the meeting or the issue being discussed.

Whatever the motivation or beliefs behind this behaviour, this company could argue that it must work because it is clearly a successful business. Leaders in this organization might even say that if more companies allowed emails in meetings they could be this successful too.

I would suggest that this company is successful despite this behaviour and not because of it.

Leadership and management are hard to measure. Leaders and managers don't always have an accurate view of their strengths and weaknesses. Leaders and managers aren't always great at judging the strengths and weakness of those around them.

So where does this leave you? Based on what I have described, you cannot know whether you are doing a good job, so how on earth can you grow?

The journey to being a great leader-manager is never-ending. You will need to read books, receive feedback (even though it has flaws), be self-analytical, watch other people you admire and, above all, experiment in real life with different approaches in order to see the results. Leadership (and management) isn't a science. It is an art. Nonetheless, even artists work hard to develop their technique. And you can too.

BE YOURSELF AND GET BETTER AT IT

Don't get too overwhelmed by these concepts of management and leadership. I have seen fabulous natural leaders become almost paralysed as they try to conform to what they perceive as the ultimate model of leadership. They twist themselves into all kinds of uncomfortable pretzel shapes in order to tick a box that says "I coach my people" or "I encourage participation" or "I am a good listener".

What Rob Goffee and Gareth Jones emphasize in *Why Should Anyone Be Led by You?* is that there are no universal leadership characteristics:

> "What works for one leader will not work for another. We think that those aspiring to leadership need to discover what it is about themselves that they can mobilize in a leadership context. They need to identify and deploy their own personal leadership assets."[7]

This means that your best hope of being a great leader-manager artist is to be yourself, but a little bit better. Where many great individuals get into trouble is that they feel pressured to be something they are not. In fact, all they need to do is develop who and what they already are. You will hear a lot about "authentic leadership", but this is all it means. When you are yourself:

1. Your words and actions are consistent. You don't have to consciously focus on making sure you "walk the talk" because in being yourself you do this naturally.

2. There is a consistency to your style. Even though different situations may bring out different behaviours, you (and other people) can see there is an underlying thread to everything you do.

3. You are comfortable with yourself. To do this you must know and accept yourself. If you do not know yourself or you do not accept yourself, you cannot display characteristics 1 and 2 above.

The good news is that you can do these three things without being particularly senior. They have nothing to do with where you sit in the hierarchy or your job title. In addition, by being this way you will attract followers (or certainly advocates and supporters) and become a leader, with influence and authority, beyond the title you hold. You will be seen as a natural leader, which can only be good for your career.

You may have concerns about being yourself. What if people find you too energetic? What if people think you are too confident? What if other people start feeling intimidated by you?

It all comes back to point 3. You need to be comfortable with yourself. You need to know what drives you and how that benefits not only you, but your people and your organization. If being yourself means you are in direct conflict with what your company stands for or the culture which predominates, and this means you feel out of place, you may need to go somewhere else. It is not a sign of failure to recognize that you are a bad fit. As you know, I left the BBC to start my own business because it became clear that being myself was a bad fit with the organizational culture. I was becoming interested in self-development and coaching and I felt these were foreign concepts in my workplace. My attempts to bring myself and the organization together were unsuccessful and I realized that I was better suited to the world of business than broadcasting.

When friends told me how brave I was to leave the security of the BBC, I could only reply that staying would be braver. To dedicate yourself to a company which constrains you from being yourself took a courage I did not possess. The easier option, in my view, was to create a business which allowed me to flex my muscles and test out my beliefs and newly discovered talents.

It is rather early in this book to suggest that you pack it all in and work somewhere else. But it is worth knowing that you always have this option.

At the same time, leaving your job could be the coward's way out. Unless you have consistently been yourself, faced the obstacles and used every opportunity to bring about change, you may well find yourself facing the very same problems in your next role.

The change must begin with you. Unless you take your self-development and your self-awareness seriously you will never really know whether the problem is the culture of your organisation or whether the problem is you.

Paul Currah has some tough words about this:

> "Don't be a victim. Don't be 'done to'. Shape your own future. Because there is a lot in any organization that is not as it should be. Those that take the view 'Let's see what we can do to change it' are likely to be more successful all around and therefore happier and fulfilled than those who say 'This is rubbish, but it's not my job to do anything about it'."

Ian Hill has been working through these challenges throughout his management career. And he says that, in doing so, he has discovered a great deal about himself and other people:

"I have learnt a lot about my character since getting into management, what makes me tick, how little I understand certain people. When you start in management you hope and feel the world must work in the way you think it works, your commitment, drive, interests. There is a real struggle to understand why other people don't have those. Over time I've got a better understanding of why other people think and behave the way they do. I've learnt a lot about my ambitions, how far I am prepared to go and the limits of my character. I think it stretches you a little more than not being in management in terms of understanding who you are."

Being a great leader-manager is about being a great person. People don't want to follow a cardboard cut-out. They want to work alongside someone real. Despite the obstacles in your way, the journey towards being "the real you" is one you can start taking right now.

UNDERSTAND WHAT DRIVES OTHER PEOPLE

Of course, as Ian Hill pointed out, knowing yourself is only part of the equation. Knowing other people is fundamental too.

Clearly, explaining how other people tick could be a whole book in itself. There is plenty of great work on motivation, on personality profiles and, of course, psychology and, as a leader-manager, the more of this you can familiarize yourself with the better. The more you know about what makes other people tick, the more precisely you can communicate with them and tap into their whole selves.

However, there are some principles which I find it very useful to know about when it comes to dealing with other people.

Don't make assumptions about other people

Life teaches us all sorts of lessons. From every experience we have, we make meaning. This becomes what my business partner at Taming Tigers, Jim Lawless, and I call our "Rulebook". We all create a "guide to life", starting very early when we are trying to understand what on earth is going on when Mum and Dad argue or when we ask for something and we don't get it. We continue to build on this "guide to life" when we go to school and learn new lessons – don't seem too intelligent in front of your friends, don't seem too keen to learn, wear the same clothes as everyone else unless you want to be bullied, there is a right and a wrong answer to everything. And we add to this Rulebook when we join the workforce. We learn to adapt to the culture rather than question it. We decide the best way to lead a team is by being tough-hearted. We start to believe we can prove our worth by staying late.

But every part of this Rulebook is based on assumption. Whenever you speculate about someone else's motivation you are making an assumption. You may believe you aren't speculating at all. You know "people like that". You can "just tell" what she's like. And, often, you can even argue "I've worked with this person for 10 years. I should know them by now".

And, maybe, your assumptions are accurate. But unless you question them you are operating in the dark. When I have a workshop to facilitate I try not to let assumptions influence me. This is why I always want to speak to some of the delegates before the day of the session. This is in addition to receiving a full brief from HR or whoever has brought us in to do the work.

This is because the official brief is often based on some amount of speculation and assumption. The HR person may assume the delegates have a higher or lower level of experience than they do. The team leader may have an idea of the problems facing the team but not the whole picture. Every delegate has their own perspective on what they want to get from the workshop and their own issues to overcome.

The official brief gives me one view. Talking to the delegates gives me 15 views. It is time-consuming and sometimes I wonder if it is overkill. But when I see the disparity between the brief and the interviews with the delegates, I feel relieved that I spent the time really listening and understanding and not buying in to the assumptions (however well-meaning) of one or two people.

As a leader-manager, you have a responsibility to question your assumptions about other people. Doing this requires listening with an open mind and really hearing what you are being told. If you assume a team member is just lazy and call her in for a one-to-one, your questions will simply reinforce your belief. It will be almost impossible for that person to convince you otherwise. However, if you wonder why someone isn't performing and stop yourself from making that leap which says "She must just be lazy", your one-to-one will be more fruitful. You will be seeking understanding. What you discover may be negative. Perhaps she is trying to take the salary without delivering any work. Perhaps she is lacking the skills to do the job. Or perhaps she is struggling with an issue at home. Maybe she is unclear about the direction of the business and can't prioritize as a result. Maybe you have communicated conflicting messages which have left her unsure of what her role is.

Questioning your assumptions about people does not mean that you accept any behaviour and become a pushover. But seeking to understand by setting aside those assumptions and listening to the other person's reality will give you a more accurate picture. It is against this accurate picture that you will be taking decisions, rather than speculation.

Differentiate between intrinsic motivators and hygiene factors

Everyone has their own reasons for going to work. Everyone has their own reasons for choosing a particular career and a particular job in a particular company. And everyone has their own reasons for feeling engaged and enthusiastic about their job or not.

Your ability to discover what these are and capitalize on them is part of your management responsibility. As you get to know your people you will become clearer about the unique combination of factors which drive them. However, there are also some common factors which most of us share – qualities we look for in a job which, if they are absent, cause us to slack off, lose confidence and even rebel.

People get confused about the role of money in motivation. They can't understand how someone who is well paid could lack motivation. But money is fundamentally a hygiene factor. What that means is that beyond a certain basic level, increasing salary reduces job dissatisfaction but doesn't increase motivation. According to work by Frederick Herzberg and others over the past 60 or more years, job satisfaction and job dissatisfaction are not opposites of each other. If you fix the factors that people complain about (work conditions, status, salary, company policy and administration, for instance), you don't get job satisfaction. You just get less job dissatisfaction.

To tap in to someone's motivation you need to appeal to their intrinsic motivators, and these six motivators are shared by most of us to a greater or lesser extent.

1. *Achievement* – people are motivated when they have a sense of achievement. If they turn up every day but have no sense of forward movement or completion, they start to lose motivation.

2. *Recognition* – people thrive when they know that their efforts have been seen and appreciated. You don't need to throw an awards ceremony to tap in to this motivator. Saying a meaningful thank you will often suffice.

3. *The work itself* – by and large people get a sense of satisfaction from doing their job. This is true no matter how menial the role. Work seems to be good for us.

4. *Responsibility* – it might frighten some people to be given responsibility and in the short term they may struggle with it. But over the longer term responsibility is motivating. We like having some ownership over what we do and seeing the results of our labours.

5. *Advancement* – in a very flat organizational structure or in a small business, the opportunities to advance through the ranks are limited. In time, this starts to matter as people wonder where they are going to go next. Seeing progress in their career is motivational.

6. *Growth* – although change is a struggle for some, change requires us to grow and growth is good for motivation. If there is no opportunity to grow people become bored and stagnate.

Organizations are very good at zapping motivation. They don't do it intentionally (why would they?), but the structures of organizations get in the way of the primary factors which motivate us. For example, if your day is dominated by answering emails it is hard to enjoy the work itself. You spend so little time doing it. Because companies are risk averse they are reluctant to give someone greater responsibility, in case they make a mistake. Senior leaders find change unsettling, so they tend to scale down their plans and minimize the opportunity for everyone in the business to grow.

As a leader-manager who wants to really change how people work, you will need to look at how the organization gets in the way of the six innate motivators. If all efforts to improve work are focused on hygiene factors, you won't be surprised to see that they aren't getting the desired results.

Focusing on innate motivators will feel strange for you and for your people. They may be suspicious. If you give more responsibility without increasing pay, you may get some resistance. Your own Rulebook might come in to play, telling you that no one is going to take on more responsibility unless they get more money. But all the evidence shows that "job enrichment" (which is what this is sometimes called) results initially in a reduction in productivity and then an improvement in productivity over and above the level at the start.

Know if your people are "towards" or "away from"

Are you more motivated towards a goal or away from a problem? Before you answer, just consider a few examples:

1. When you left your last job, did you do it because you disliked it or because you had already found something better?
2. When you moved house, did you do it primarily because you wanted to get out of the home you were in or because you had an ideal in mind?
3. When you think about taking time off, do you look forward to it because of all the things you'll be doing or because of all the things you will stop doing?

Most of us are a combination of "away from" and "towards" motivated, but we have a predominant style. There is nothing better about being "towards" motivated, even though a lot of people think so. Being "away from" does not mean you are negative. Nelson Mandela spoke of an end to apartheid but he was not being negative, just appealing to the "away from" motivators in his audience.

When you communicate, it is useful to have a sense of whether the people you are speaking to are "away from" or "towards" motivated. Telling an "away from" person all the advantages of the new way of working won't be as powerful as reminding her of all the things she will be leaving behind.

It also helps to understand when you are listening. When someone in your team says "I have found three problems which need to be resolved before we can move on", you won't see them as disrupting your plans. Instead you will appreciate that they are "away from" and so cannot get behind the plan until they have resolved how the problems are going to be fixed. When someone in your team says "Let's just go for it", you won't think they haven't taken the problems seriously just that, as a "towards" person, keeping the ultimate aim alive is what keeps them focused.

Understand and capitalize on work-style preferences

Everyone has their own work-style preference. Some of us are more structured – we have tidy desks, neat calendars and are always early for meetings. Others are more comfortable with flexibility – their desks are a mess and they are often late, but they cope very well during change and don't get stressed by surprises. Some people like detail, others like the big picture. Some people enjoy sifting through data before they make a decision, others go with their gut.

A work-style preference isn't the same as a skill. You may be very skilled at something which isn't a preference. And the reverse is true too. So, I am quite creative. I come up with new ideas with ease. My preference is for creative work and once the "new ideas" bit of the project is done I lose interest fast. But I am not a talented artist. I am not skilled at that. On the other hand, whilst I prefer not to do detailed tasks and like the big picture, I have learnt the skill of completing the book. It isn't my natural preference, but I have developed a necessary skill.

It can be hard to separate preference from skill, especially because you may be very skilled at something *because* you have innate preference for that way of working or you may be very skilled at something *because* you had to work extra hard at it.

If you are finding it hard to identify your preferences, consider what you like to do and how you like to do it outside of work. (You can also apply this test when trying to identify the skills and preferences of your team.)

Are you a bit of a performer (which would suggest you are more extrovert) or do you prefer to spend time alone working on a project (which might suggest you are more introvert)? Do you have a very organized filing system or are your papers in disarray? Do you consult expert websites and publications before making a purchase or buy based on instinct?

Another way to identify a preference is to think back to childhood. What were the activities where you got lost in the moment? What were you doing and how were you doing it? Whilst preferences can change over a lifetime, looking back to your past may provide clues and help you differentiate between a preference and a skill.

But why is it important to know your own preferences? Why is it important to differentiate them from a skill? And how important is it to know the preferences of the people around you?

If you are going to be yourself, self-knowledge is fundamental. When we are under pressure, our natural preferences tend to come out more strongly. You may be able to cope day to day with work which is out of alignment with your preferences, but during times of organizational change, high stress or tight deadlines, your natural preferences leak out. This can be a problem to those around you who have come to see you a certain way. If, generally, you are well-organized and decisive, your peers, line managers and direct reports will come to expect this of you. However, if under pressure you become disorganized and indecisive, it is hard for them to know how to relate to you. Unpredictability is not an admirable quality in a leader.

This doesn't mean you should give up the fight and be disorganized and indecisive all the time. Just be aware of your tendency, keep other people informed about what to expect, and see if you can get extra support during high-pressure times to minimize your Jekyll and Hyde behaviour. During high-pressure times I put my PA in charge of all my emails and admin and I focus on the jobs only I can do. Whilst I can cope day to day with the detail of admin and email, under pressure my preference for big picture work comes out strongly. My emergency plan kicks in and clients don't notice a difference. What's your emergency plan?

As a leader-manager, you also need to know what drives other people, so knowing how to spot different preferences is going to be helpful. You will be able to give them work which most suits their natural style and, when it is necessary for them to do work which isn't a preference for them, you will be able to spot the early signs of stress. When people are expected to work for long periods outside their preferences they experience greater levels of stress. Whilst it is good for people to stretch themselves beyond their comfort zone in order to grow, stretching doesn't influence innate preferences. No matter how much detailed work I do, I will never have a preference for it. Don't impose a form of aversion therapy on your people. If you want to keep them and help them to thrive, support them to work in ways which match their preferences for as much of the time as possible.

Belinda, a manager in the NHS, thinks that this ability to empathize and adapt to the personalities of the people we work with is going to be increasingly important as a quality of leader-managers:

"I think we are going to need empathetic leaders in future. An ideal leader-manager would be able to work with almost anyone in their team and get good work out of them. You need to be able to listen and know what makes people tick. Not all people work as you do, so you need to be able to set objectives that always contain an element of something that's going to get that person excited. Also, you need to be a fluent communicator. You need to get your team excited, remind them what they are doing is important. It can be difficult in the middle of a project when you see all the bad stuff that is kicking off. You have to show the potential impact of carrying on."

WHAT SHOULD A LEADER-MANAGER DO ALL DAY?

All this is very well but you've got a job to do. I mean, who is going to write that proposal, go to that sales meeting, keep up with all the phone calls and email, complete the spreadsheet and all the other myriad activities you are meant to be doing all day? If you spend all your day managing and leading people, how is any of the real work going to get done?

My view is that managing and leading people *is* the real work. Most job descriptions don't recognize this, so you probably do have other expectations to fulfil. But even if 70% of your time is taken up with non-management activity, your *head* should be in a leader-manager state of mind.

Think "We". At the same time as emailing, printing documents out and listening to voice mail, you need to be constantly thinking "We" rather than "I". Leadership guru, Peter Drucker, says "This one may sound simple; it isn't, but it needs to be strictly observed".[8]

No matter what you are doing, ask yourself who you are doing it for. Are you doing it for the good of the organization or for the good of the people in the organization? Or are you doing it for yourself? One of the most significant stands you can make if you want to make work work better is to ask "Who is this good for?" Are you involved in a paper-shuffling exercise or are you adding value to the organization? Are you just ticking a box or are you making a difference?

John Barnes says this may involve asking quite direct questions of your line management:

"I think you have to take the time to ask the questions and the smart thing is to ask the question in a round about way so you aren't seen as saying 'You are the problem aren't you?' For example, a good question might be 'If we complete this in the way you've asked me to complete it, what is going to be different?' And when they tell you what is going to be different, you ask them 'So, what's the value of that?' and then you might get to what the problem really is."

Make decisions. If you have got to the end of the day without making a firm decision you haven't been doing what a leader does. A leader is making decisions all day.

This decisiveness is very important to Belinda:

"You need to be clear, not woolly at all. There is nothing more frustrating than people who are woolly or indecisive. You need to have balls to make decisions. If they are wrong that's ok but you need the confidence to take action within 24 hours of an issue coming up. As a manager you are turning strategy into action so you need to be able to break ideas into tasks. And you need to trust your team to do their job properly. You make a commitment that if they screw up you will take the flak but in return you have to say 'The payback is you have to tell me the instant you are worried about something, so I am never up there defending you without information'."

Being decisive includes deciding who is going to be accountable for each action and who needs to be informed and consulted. You can't just leave this to chance. Even if you anticipate delegating a task completely, make sure these aspects are done. Otherwise you haven't fully delegated and your "decision" won't stick.

Communicate. If information stops at you, you are an obstacle to the success of the business rather than a powerful tool in that success. You are in a position to pass relevant information up, relevant information down, and to seek answers to questions that will otherwise get overlooked or lost somewhere between the top of the company and the bottom. This requires communication. John Barnes expects his managers to be communicating with him constantly, just as he communicates with his. Most importantly, he wants to know what is important and what is not working well. He doesn't want just the good news:

"I like my line reports to do what I do for my line managers – work through all the detail, simplify the detail and stratify it so the difficult stuff and the things that are not going to plan come to the top. If they aren't able to manage an issue themselves I will step in, in a way that is intended to be invisible and if it is really out of control I may take it over. A lot of people don't give you the very early information that something is not going right or they wait for it to go wrong and then come to you. Or they wait for you to find out it's gone wrong and explain it to you. Not quite enough anxiety gets shared. That's because people think it reflects badly

Continued

on them if things aren't going perfectly. You try to ensure people don't get penalized for telling you the truth and they get more penalized if they don't share it with you but the system doesn't work perfectly. I only bite when I don't know what's going on."

Seek and develop talent. As a leader-manager, as much time as possible should be invested in developing your people and developing yourself. You are aiming for a world where you are surrounded by people who are better than you. Try not to feel threatened by this scenario. It won't make you defunct. The fact that you have been able to do this – to transform a team and harness everything those people have to offer – will make you more valuable than any other leader in your company.

Self-development applies to you too. Your own team should have strengths and preferences which balance your own. And you will also want to seek counsel and development from people outside your own team – mentors, friends and former colleagues.

Graham Massey has managed teams in the corporate world and in his own smaller business. He says being a manager has taught him one lesson above all, the importance of being able to take advice:

"Surround yourself by people better than you, which is hard to do when egos get in the way. A lot of business owners need to understand cash flow and a lot of successful businesses go out of business because they run out of cash. I think that is why it is important to have a mentor from early on. The banks and all that officialdom won't navigate you through that. We should have had a mentor and we didn't."

THE ROLE OF EMOTIONS

I was recently involved in a conversation with a group of fellow leaders, discussing the place of emotion in the workplace. The debate centred on whether it was useful for a leader to share his emotions with his line reports or whether that might intimidate or even just confuse the poor employee.

It seems strange to me that some emotions are encouraged in the workplace while others are seen as evil. It is not acceptable to show anger but it is acceptable to show joy. It is not acceptable to show doubt but it is acceptable to show confidence. It is not acceptable to show disappointment but it is acceptable to show recognition.

It is partly this perceived "ban" on certain emotions which makes leaders seem inhuman (even inhumane). When leaders are seen as out of reach it is difficult to learn from them, to communicate with them, to satisfy them or to aspire to be like them. Above all, it is hard to trust them.

But there is some evidence that there is a place for emotions at work, even the "bad" ones.

Conflict is a good example. Conflict is seen as "bad". When we find ourselves in conflict we often raise our voice (or if voices aren't raised our blood pressure is), we find ourselves arguing heatedly and we feel frustrated that people disagree. This can make other people who witness this conflict feel uncomfortable. And we can take this conflict home and suffer a sleepless night wondering how we can get past the conflict to a consensual decision.

However, there is a powerful case for conflict and argument in the workplace. Without it, sparks are not created and new ideas do not emerge. In a team where everyone finds consensus all the time there is very little innovation.

One of the theories behind the collapse of financial services company, Lehman Brothers, is that there was too much harmony. Although there were signs that the business was in trouble, people inside the business were too afraid to point this out for fear of being seen as trouble-makers. Loyalty was considered more important.[9]

Take a look at two of the most famous business people of our time – Bill Gates and Steve Ballmer at Microsoft. Apparently they are well known for raising their voices. At Goldman Sachs the environment is not one of politeness and respect but one of competition and driving hard. At Sysco, the food distributor, managers are regularly penalized for failing to meet their productivity targets. Such cultures don't feel nice and comfortable. They are full of conflict and argument.

According to the authors of *How to Pick a Good Fight*, "… it's time to stop candy-coating what's taught to executives and their direct reports. It's time to stop pretending that conflict-free teamwork is the be-all and end-all of organisational life".[10]

Don't misunderstand. This isn't carte-blanche to become a bully. It doesn't mean a lot of backstabbing and gossip. This is about having the *right* fights, out in the open, with your true emotions on display. It is another form of the authenticity we discussed at the start of this chapter.

In any case, it is very hard to keep your emotions under wraps. They leak out when you least expect it (shouting at your partner when you get home, being rude to a customer who did nothing wrong, sending a stroppy email to an unfortunate colleague). And people around you are not blind to what you are feeling. They sense it. And when you don't own up they come to doubt you. Instead of being someone honest and straightforward you become someone they have to read.

Anger and dissent aren't the only powerful emotions. Daniel Shapiro, the director of the Harvard International Negotiation Program, says that tapping in to the positive emotions of your people, even when presenting bad news, is also strong stuff. He gives the example of two employees being made redundant. One has a boss who does not express any appreciation for her years of loyalty, leaving her feeling abandoned and disconnected. She threatens to sue. Another has a boss who kept him up-to-date about the financial difficulties the business was in, asked for his suggestions about increasing revenue and, when the time eventually came to make him redundant, offered to share his network of contacts, told him he would be rehired once the business turned around and offered him the option to stay on part-time. As Shapiro puts it, "Positive emotions are a low-cost, high-payoff source of value".[11]

By facing up to the emotional realities of what your people are experiencing, you acknowledge their emotions and help them manage them in constructive ways.

Be able to name emotions

We don't have a strong vocabulary when it comes to emotions. Or, rather, there are lots of words in the dictionary to describe emotions but we rarely use them. When I ask clients how they feel I often get a reply which doesn't have anything to do with emotion.

I might ask "How did you feel when your manager said that to you?", only to hear my client respond "I felt he should have been more honest with me".

That isn't an emotion. Here are some emotions: joy, trust, fear, surprise, sadness, disgust, anger, anticipation, optimism, love, submission, awe, disappointment, aggressiveness, remorse, contempt, disgust, envy, pride, cheerfulness, relief, rage, irritation, shame, sympathy, horror, nervousness, contentment, jealousy, enthusiasm, delight ...

There isn't a shortage of words. According to research from the Maryland Business School, "Managers and employees should try to increase their emotional self-awareness and learn to describe and differentiate their feelings – especially negative ones – during decision making. Participants with a more refined ability to perceive and describe their feelings were better at preventing their emotions from biasing their decisions".[12]

By ignoring your emotions or wrongly identifying them you actually risk being misled by your feelings. No wonder we think of emotions at work as dangerous. When they are badly handled they can do harm. But when they are correctly labelled, expressed openly and used to help us communicate, they can be a powerful tool for the leader-manager.

Know when to fight

According to business strategist Saj-nicole A. Joni, an issue must pass each of these three stages in order to merit a good fight:[13]

1. Make it material – The issue should have the potential to save or make the company a significant amount (10–15% per year) or grow your sales faster than the market. The issue should be complex and routine processes, calling in expert help or

holding different parts of the business accountable for different pieces of the problem would not be enough to resolve the problem. If it is to be resolved, the solution should require the organization to change fundamentally in order for a good fight to be justified.

2. Focus on the future – If the issue is about blame for the past or working through the details of something that has already happened, there isn't a case for a good fight. Fighting should be about what is possible not what is past. If the issue presents an opportunity to innovate or create a bold vision to get people to embrace change, there may be benefits to a fight. Is the way forward very unclear during a time of dramatic change? If so, there may be a case for a fight.

3. Pursue a noble purpose – Does the challenge relate to something more than making money? Will the process of solving the challenge motivate people to go above and beyond their normal responsibilities? Will a solution to the issue win respect from stakeholders? If the answer is yes to any of these, there may be a case for a good fight.

If you believe your issue meets these criteria, you need to also ensure that the fight will be fair. This isn't a charter for outdoing your opponents. It is about shaking things up and boosting your staff's energy and creativity for a noble cause.

Listen to inklings

Something most of us are bad at is trusting our instincts. Often we knew months before the crisis point that there was a problem brewing but we ignored our inklings in an effort to see both sides of the story, or because we wanted to trust the words of one of our people (even though their deeds conflicted with those words), or because we were reassured by people around us that everything would turn out fine.

Clearly, you will want to be open to outside views and demonstrate trust in your people. At the same time, ignoring your feelings is pointless. As we have seen, they leak out anyway. And expressing them, if done correctly, has very little negative impact.

Let's say you have asked one of your direct reports to finish a piece of work by the end of the month. Within a few days you start to get a bad feeling. Some of the early phases of that piece of work have not yet been started. The direct report seems overwhelmed by other tasks and you are starting to worry.

You could say "Bill, you're not going to make that deadline at this rate". But this may not be powerful enough feedback for Bill. He is likely to just reassure you that everything is fine.

Alternatively, you could talk about your feelings, the facts and your needs.

When you talk about feelings, start the sentence with "I feel …" followed by a word which describes an emotion. Then give the facts. And then be very clear about what you need.

For example, "Bill, I feel really worried. By this stage you agreed to make that phone call and reconfigure the spreadsheet and neither have been done yet. I need to know when those steps are going to be taken and any obstacles in your way".

This isn't guaranteed to work on its own. You may need to continue expressing your emotions, backed up with facts and clarifying your needs, until the message gets through. However, what this does achieve is clarity and honesty about your expectations. It also punctuates your point with an emotion. Bill does not want you to be worried. He wants you to be reassured. Now he knows that telling you everything will be fine is not going to reassure you. But seeing that the phone call has been made and the spreadsheet has been reconfigured will reassure you. Now, if he doesn't do it, you are likely to have some even stronger emotions to share with him.

Ultimately, a penalty for failure to achieve the expressed outcome will need to be identified, e.g., "Bill, I feel frustrated. This is the third time we have had a conversation where I tell you what I need and still you haven't made progress. I need to see at least three steps taken by the end of the week or I am going to reassign this project to Jill".

These aren't just words. This isn't a technique. It is a way to accurately express your emotions (and the facts and your needs) in order to be very, very clear. Prepare by thinking about what emotions you are actually experiencing, identify the facts and know in your own mind what your needs are. Then let your emotions show rather than reading this like a script, and see if it makes any difference.

MIS-LEADERSHIP – FINAL THOUGHTS

Being an exceptional leader-manager covers a huge array of skills. It is a multi-facetted job and, chances are, your actual job spec doesn't cover most of what is really required to be successful.

However, as a leader-manager, you have a great opportunity. You have a powerful role in creating the culture of the business. The style of the leader impacts the climate (the feel of the place) by between 50–70%. And organizational climate impacts results by up to 28%.[14] If anyone claims this is all HR stuff and has nothing to do with the successful operation of the business, these are some useful numbers to reflect back. It is also worth remembering that one of the main reasons people leave their job (or stay, for that matter) is their relationship with their direct manager.[15] Although you might not see models of leadership or management in your company, there is a huge benefit to shifting your perceptions and enhancing the working lives of your direct line reports, even if that requires being a lone voice for a period of time. But as you start to see the results in your part of the business, you start to create a powerful case for change at a wider level.

Of course, change doesn't just happen. You need to know where you are going. And you need to have some ideas about how you are going to get there. And that's where Vision comes in. Unfortunately, it seems as if some companies are having a little trouble with their eyesight. Let's find out why.

Frustration 3:
Blurred Vision

I've been meeting members of the finance team at a medium-sized business in the City of London for most of the day. I have sat in on team briefings, talked to team members one-to-one and heard from the manager about some of the performance problems she has been noticing.

A few people have mentioned that team work seems to be breaking down. Some say that they aren't sure what their job is and expectations of them seem to change daily. Others say there are tensions between the newer members of the team and the longer-serving ones. One or two say it used to be much more enjoyable when the company was smaller and less well-established. Others say they don't know what is going on and wonder if the people at the top do. One member of the team is feeling particularly hard done by and confides that she is probably going to leave because she finds the work boring and repetitive. This is all the more disheartening because she thought she was joining a vibrant company on the growth curve and was promised opportunities to be part of the success of the business. Lots of minor but grating annoyances are mentioned to me – problems with communication, problems with the online database, problems with specific team members, problems with staff in other teams, unrealistic targets, lack of understanding by "the management" about the pressure everyone is under, long hours. I am filling up my notepad with grievances.

The manager takes all of these complaints seriously but is overwhelmed by the thought of trying to fix everything. The unhappiness of her team is keeping her awake at night and she looks frazzled. At the same time she is frustrated that her team haven't taken the initiative and set about resolving some of the problems themselves. They are intelligent, experienced people. Why don't they take some ownership instead of complaining all the time? She wonders, perhaps in desperation, whether they just need a team-building day to pull everyone together and suggests that I take them all to a High Ropes centre in Yorkshire.

Sometimes, in a team where some of the fun seems to have disappeared and a fresh injection of energy is required, a day out is all that is needed.

But usually there is a deeper issue at the heart of these kinds of observations and feelings. When I see lots of seemingly unrelated complaints, concerns and frictions, everyone with their own view of what is wrong and what needs to be fixed, I look for the common denominator. It is very unlikely that there are 20 unrelated problems going on simultaneously in a team. That would be rather bad luck, wouldn't it? No, it is far more likely that they have one or perhaps two root causes and that, unless we get to the real issue, dealing with the symptoms won't change anything. Those problems may go away but new ones will pop up in their place.

The most common core problem a team like this is experiencing is "Blurred Vision". A direction, an over-riding sense of momentum towards a goal which is meaningful to everyone, a definition of what success would look like, feel like, smell like … none of these are clear. On a day-to-day basis, people get on with what sits in their inbox and what lands on their desk. They may have annual targets to hit or objectives set out during their performance appraisal. But there is no sense of shared purpose, shared mission, shared vision. Related to this, people aren't clear about how they contribute to the success of the business. They don't know how they play a part or even if they play a part. They do their best, given the information they have, but that information is short-sighted and often contradictory. This week they are told to focus on customer relationships but last week they were told to focus on up-selling to current customers and last month they were told to bring in new business at all costs. They are only ever able to react to the problems of the moment, because there is no broader perspective.

When people don't know where they are heading and how they are going to get there, they can't be proactive. How can you take initiative when you don't know what the bigger picture is? How can you come up with ideas for growing the business or improving the way the team operates if you don't know what the business or team is trying to become? It is inevitable that you get bogged down by fire-fighting and in-fighting.

And, on top of that, if you are a manager, how can you rally the people who work for you, get them facing in the same direction and working together to solve problems when you are just as clueless about what the business expects from you beyond meeting targets or coming in on budget? All you can do is give it your best guess and hope you've done what the guys upstairs want.

Without a clear vision (and we will come to what this really means shortly), teams start to fall apart and petty problems start to dominate everyone's working hours.

WHY DO COMPANIES (AND TEAMS ... AND THEREFORE MANAGERS) NEED A DIRECTION?

Troubleshooter, John Harvey Jones wrote that, "The business that is not being purposefully led in a clear direction which is understood by its people is not going to survive, and all of history shows that that is the case".[1]

His view, based on his years at ICI as chairman (and his career working his way up from humble beginnings) is that managing the status quo is dangerous. Your competitors have you marked as an easy target if all your company does is keep ticking over, making marginal improvements to profit or turnover every year. Within a five-year period it is likely, according to Harvey-Jones, that "the business is not alright unless something has been done about it".[2] In other words, as leader-managers we must constantly be looking at what we are doing, how we are doing it and for what end. If we don't we will find, eventually, when serious and fundamental problems start surfacing, that things were not as good as we thought.

The danger when a business waits for problems to emerge, rather than taking a proactive approach to the future, is that what started as a few seemingly minor problems turns into a mass of small, medium-sized and huge problems which overwhelm the managers in the company. As increasing sick leave, poor performance, loss of morale, deteriorating customer service, tensions between teams and within teams, lack of consistency, lack of drive and enthusiasm and high staff turnover (for instance) start dominating everyone's time and attention, the temptation is to handle the issues that have arisen individually. So, if customer service has been revealed as a problem, customer-facing staff are sent on a training course, given a new set of guidelines and set some fresh targets. The hope is to quickly resolve the issue because poor customer service is obviously very bad for business. There is no time to lose. Who knows how long customers have been complaining about the customer complaints department?

This sends a message to managers in the organization to do the same. When you see a problem, resolve it. Fast. And keep solving problems until such time as you have resolved them all and can return to life as normal. Occasionally you will even be told that the company is planning to look at the future direction of the business when all these "little problems" are resolved. Except that, when you are constantly fixing problems as they arise, you never get to "life as normal". Your life becomes a vicious cycle of fixing problems which, you suspect, are interconnected but you haven't the time to step back and take a longer, in-depth look.

I have nothing against "quick wins". If there are problems which can be quickly resolved and get you a big bang for your buck, go ahead. But if the only strategy is quick wins, the fundamental causes which led to these problems in the first place are never revealed or addressed.

In my experience, these problems were created (and ignored) as a result of short-term thinking. Without a vision it is inevitable that people in a business look only at what lies directly in front of their faces. They don't consider what is lying around the corner. If short-term thinking created the problem, short-term thinking isn't going to resolve it. What is needed is a clear and compelling direction (or vision) which remains fixed, even when events threaten to take the business off course, and which provides everyone with the context for the disruption they see around them.

WHAT IS A VISION?

I am sure you've heard leaders in your company talk about its vision, its mission, its purpose and/or its values. We hear these words a lot at work but they all seem to mean the same thing (or they seem to mean nothing). So let's clarify some terms.

Vision – The vision describes how an organization finds its fulfilment. It "declares the company's intention with regard to the future it desires to create".[3] It is a statement of the overall goal. If there was ever a finishing line, the vision describes what it should look like to win gold in the race.

The vision does not change. It is sacred. It defines what is core about the company and what future it is aiming for.

Back in the 1950s, electronics company Sony set out a very clear vision – "To become the company most known for changing the worldwide poor-quality image of Japanese products".

The company wanted "Made in Japan to mean something fine, not something shoddy". It is hard now to remember a time when "Made in Japan" meant anything different.

This is what a vision is meant to do. It pulls together the company's core values and purpose and, with a vivid description of what the 10- to 30-year goal is, presents a picture of the future which is coherent and compelling to everyone.

It should talk to employees and to society, and it should resonate with that audience. This sounds like a lot, but it can be summed up in a pithy sentence or paragraph. In fact, if it is going to work you should be able to say it without taking a breath (or fainting afterwards).

Mission – This declares the company's core business. This is important in any company, but is particularly important where the products and services provided by that company seem diverse. Of course, the mission statement doesn't have to say of a furniture company "We Make Chairs". It can be a bit more imaginative – such as the mission statement of Steelcase, who provide office furniture, which is "Helping people work more effectively". This describes what the company does for its customers. What its customers get isn't just a chair; it is a tool to help them work more effectively.

Avis car rental also has a mission statement, which describes what it does and what it aims to do for customers – "Our business is renting cars; our mission is total customer satisfaction".

Would you be able to describe what your company's mission was (without checking the intranet site)? And (now you have checked), does that mission align with the priorities that fill your diary? If you don't know what the mission is, if there isn't a mission, or if there is a mission but it is out of sync with the way the company operates, there is a fundamental problem to resolve. It may not be within your remit to resolve it at its core, but there are some steps you can take to create a mission for your own part of the business or just for your small team.

Remember that the mission (also known as "the purpose") should be inspirational to the people who need to be inspired. It isn't meant to appeal specifically to investors or shareholders. So talking about profits or turnover probably isn't particularly relevant.

Values – These provide the rules of behaviour or standards of the organization. They are the deeply held beliefs which inform the right way of "being" when you work at that company. And by establishing the company's values you create a code of behaviour that binds people together and supports the vision and mission. The values show people how they are expected to go about delivering the mission and achieving the vision. They provide guidance which tells staff "We don't achieve our mission and vision at any cost. We achieve them by behaving in a certain way".

Of course, all companies have values, whether they are overtly recognized or not. Those values may be positive and support the exact behaviours the company needs to see in order to achieve its vision. Or they may be negative and undermine the company's ability to achieve its vision. Think about the company you work in. What are the condoned ways of being? Are you encouraged and supported in being honest? Or is honesty really a rather relative term in your company, which only means that you say the truth unless saying the truth is going to get you into trouble or upset someone?

Does your business genuinely care about its corporate social responsibility in the sense that the impact of decisions on the local community, the environment and the planet are taken into account? Or does it say it cares about these issues but, in fact, values expansion and shareholder returns more?

If you were being brutally honest, what values do you think your company really operates by? And what values does your team operate by? Yes, the one you manage. I do not doubt you have some great people and a lovely time when you go for drinks together. I am just asking how the team behaves in the way it does business. Is it honest? Does it put integrity first? Does it strive for excellence in everything? Does it reward initiative?

My intention isn't to suggest your team members have a dubious set of personal values. Only that, in the workplace, it is often hard to keep hold of those values. The workplace has the power to suffocate them and replace them with far less admirable beliefs and behaviours.

We've explored beliefs before, so you know how powerful they can be if they are not recognized. For example, a belief that you must keep a client at all costs may translate into a behaviour which prioritizes the client over the well-being of your colleagues. However, sometimes it is not worth keeping a client at any cost. The price your people are paying for dealing with that individual or that organization is too great. In order to put that client first, your people may have to compromise their own integrity daily. They may have to lie, they may have to kowtow, they may have to be demanding of their colleagues – knowing what they are asking for goes beyond what is reasonable. If you and your company claim to "put employees first" or that "our people are our most important asset", that means that, when push comes to shove, employees should take precedence over clients. However it is a brave company, a forward-thinking company, which embraces what valuing their people really means.

Bland values

One of the problems with company values is how bland they are. They normally include "honesty and integrity" and something about "doing good in the world", "respecting each other" and "quality in everything we do". And all these are worthy values. They may even be a true reflection of what the company does stand for. The issue I have with them is that these should be taken for granted in a sense. Write them down by all means. But it isn't these values which really make your company culture stand out. It isn't these values which will give you the edge over your competition. And it isn't these values which will attract or help you keep the best people.

You can argue that "honesty and integrity" might be the stated values of many companies but your company really means it. That may be true too. But what if you were to be more ambitious? What if you were to set the bar higher?

Vision experts James Collins and Jerry Porras write that you must "push with relentless honesty to define what values are truly central. If you can articulate more than five or six, chances are that you are confusing core values (which do not change) with operating practices, business strategies or cultural norms".[4]

You can demand high-quality products, respect for colleagues and making a profit, and these can be spelt out in your business strategy or in your staff contracts. But they aren't distinctive enough to be core values.

VISION MINUS COMMUNICATION EQUALS DANGER

Some companies haven't invested any time in consciously creating a vision, mission or clarifying their values. Most, though, have brought in some external consultants to do this job. Not that you would necessarily know. Because having vision, mission and values is not enough. Even if your organization has a fabulous and inspirational Vision Statement on the home page of its website, there are still a number of problems that can prevent it having meaning to people in the business. For one, it needs to be communicated properly to the people who matter – the employees.

Your leadership team may have spent a week locked in a conference room thrashing out the vision and the strategy required to achieve that vision and return to work ready to bring it to life, but they will fail to inspire and invigorate their people if the rest of the organization is unaware of the vision, knows about it but doesn't believe in it, or thinks the vision is flawed.

Without clear, consistent communication about what the vision is, why it is important, what it means for the people who work in the organization, how it is going to be brought to fruition and unless they see real commitment to the vision from their leaders, employees are left in a vacuum. And vacuums are very bad news.

Let's say the company leadership has developed a grand vision, taking into account input from staff, conversations with clients and a full awareness of the needs of other stakeholders. And let's say that turning this vision into reality requires some difficult decisions, one of which is to cut head count (make job losses, in other words).

When a company starts firing people (or recruiting people or setting up an innovation department or relocating staff to new desks or refurbishing the canteen), this can be unsettling for all staff. They ask, "What does this mean?" And, if that question isn't answered, speculation follows.

The rumour machine in most businesses works so slickly that it eats official communication for breakfast. The chief executive makes a relatively clear speech at 9am to all staff and by 5pm the message is embellished with speculation, assumption, fear and gossip. These unofficial stories are very powerful and official communication is rarely as compelling.

However, when a company has a set of core values, a core purpose and a vision which people understand and accept (or even embrace) – and which remain fixed, even during turbulent times – it is able to adapt more easily to change. If the core values and vision really resonate and have meaning for everyone in the business, and if they are reinforced everyday in terms of the style and words of the leadership, the company's practices towards its people and outside stakeholders, its approach to problems and mistakes and its role in the community, they become as powerful as any amount of gossip. Staff can always refer back to them for reassurance.

Instead of wondering whether there is a hidden agenda when they start seeing change around them, they will be reminded of the core values and purpose of the business – e.g., "Honesty and integrity" or "To provide a place for people to flourish". If the company has always shown itself to be true to these values or to this vision, it will have created a strong level of trust amongst staff. In such a healthy environment, people believe that the company acts in integrity with its stated vision and therefore they do not assume any underhanded motivation.

Karen Mellor, an experienced manager at a major pharmaceutical company, says the company vision needs to appeal to everyone in the organization:

> "For a vision to work well you should be able to look at it and know what it means for you. I am not a scientist so some pharmaceutical visions don't resonate with me. I need the translation into what we do and how we manage in order to really get it. I think that if time is spent in the organization ensuring staff really understand the company's vision then you have a much better chance of pulling in the right direction, i.e. everyone is on the right side of the rope. As many companies are, some people are pulling on one side and some are pulling on the other."

Vision/reality mis-match

Of course, a poorly communicated vision isn't the only mistake leaders can make when it comes to getting the most from Vision Statements, Mission Statements, Corporate Value Statements or whatever they choose to call them.

Once seen as a panacea, these tools have been misused and given a bad name over the years. And a common flaw is when the Vision Statement or Mission Statement does not bear any resemblance to the reality of working in the business.

In such circumstances, the vision becomes the focus of ridicule. When a company says it values honesty but then "marks the card" of anyone who speaks out against policies or decisions made by senior people, staff begin to wonder whether the stated vision and values are anything more than a public relations exercise. When a company says it wants to be carbon neutral but then removes bicycle parking spaces in order to give the CEO a reserved car-parking space, people start to question how great its commitment to the environment really is. When a company says it wants to compete on quality not price, but then sets financial targets which require a cut in quality and a focus on volume, people begin to get suspicious.

The mis-match between the vision or values and the realities of the company may not be as obvious as this. In very subtle ways – tone of voice, a raised eyebrow, favouritism, a rushed email written in a moment of anger – leaders can betray their true feelings and true priorities, feelings and priorities which do not sit comfortably with the stated vision and values that were so enthusiastically presented to the staff months before.

Obviously, the vision should be aspirational, which means it is what the company strives to be and not necessarily what it is right now. A vision might state "We want to be known for our commitment to the planet" and it may not yet have plastic bottle recycling onsite. But for a vision to be valid it should provide an intention and standard by which behaviour is measured and not be a meaningless document which is good for your public image but irrelevant to the workforce.

WHAT CAN A REAL VISION DO?

Given that creating a vision which really works is hard and there are so many pitfalls that need to be avoided in order that it isn't a huge and expensive waste of time and paper, what are the benefits? And why, as a middle manager, should any of this be important to you?

Visions provide meaning

As we have seen, people increasingly want to know how they contribute to the success of their business. Most people in a company are not delivering the service or making the product which brings in the money. They are in support services – IT, Accounting, HR, Customer Complaints, Help Desk, Facilities Management, Security, Reception, Catering, Administration. On a daily basis their focus is not on making or saving the business money. They often do not see a connection between their daily toil and the success of the business. Equally, they often do not see a connection between their mistakes, their low productivity or their overheads and problems in the business. They may be on the receiving end of policies which are intended to save money, such as voluntary redundancy, an end to bonuses or the locking of the stationery cupboard, but they cannot see how these decisions have any impact on the business. All they can see is that working life just got harder. In the worst case, it feels personal.

If you manage a team which cannot make the connection between their work and the business at large, it can be very difficult to motivate them, retain them or keep them focused on what is critical versus just being busy.

However, when a company has a strong vision, which is understood and believed by the staff, companies can bring about radical change – even change that has a negative impact on people's job security, their salary or their working conditions, with a high level of support and engagement. If you can help people see how what they do contributes to the business, and how these changes will make the business a better place to work and a more successful company, they can see why they are necessary. This is going to be a huge benefit to you as you guide and encourage your team. They will clearly see the link between what you are asking them to do and the well-being of the business.

It is what people look for in leaders

72% of employees want their leader to be "forward-looking".[5] Only 27% expect their peers to be forward-thinking. This means that, when you were an individual contributor or a team member without line responsibility, this ability to be forward-thinking was not particularly in demand. But as soon as you stepped into a management position you became expected to display this characteristic. This might explain why so many leaders are bad at it. Only 3% of the typical executive's day is spent envisioning and enlisting support. You probably spend more time reading your horoscope.

That doesn't mean you have to be the human equivalent of a time-traveller with an uncanny ability to predict the future. It means that, once you are a manager, it is your job to get everyone involved in creating the goals and buying in to the vision so it has meaning for each individual you manage. It means asking questions like, "What do we have to do to be better?" and "Who do we need to be?" Visionary leaders don't have to know all the answers, but they are expected to ask some visionary questions.

It feels great when you get there

People need some reason to stay interested in the work they do. On a daily basis, a lot of it is repetitive and humdrum. Even in a business that really works, that has addressed these Frustrations, there will be mini-frustrations and boring days. In such moments, people wonder what they are doing and why they are doing it. They may feel that life is greener somewhere else and that, now that their job has become largely second-nature, it is time to move on.

However, when people see that their organization is aiming for a big goal, they want to hang around and see that goal realized. Thomas A. Stewart, the editor of *Harvard Business Review*, wrote – "Seeing the future and getting it right feels great ... Nothing is more rewarding than completing a job well done ... The art of managing for the long term is the art of making the whole greater than the sum of its parts".[6]

If you can help your team feel part of the future of the business, they will want to stick around and work hard in order to be a small part of that success.

Jane Ginnever is responsible for coordinating and consulting on the change going on in her organization. She believes a vision lies at the heart of any change or growth strategy:

"I think a vision needs to set out where we are all heading, the long-term goal of the company. It should be aspirational and inspirational. It should be something we never achieve. This is where everyone's efforts should be directed. It draws the strings together. There are so many things going on in a business. Having a long-term vision helps create the culture you want to create and gives everyone some things to aim at. Without that, people are slogging their guts out and they don't quite know why – is it because of shareholder value or something else? People want to know they are part of something. They want to feel they are contributing towards something. I think that is a really positive thing for us all."

And that is what a great vision should do – bring all the parts of the business together into something greater.

CAN A TEAM HAVE ITS OWN VISION, MISSION AND VALUES?

So you have a part to play in bringing the company vision, if your company has one, to life for your people. But what if the company vision is meaningless or absent? What is your job then? After all, you just lead a small team within a large company and, surely, you can't be expected to transform the whole business by forcing the company to rewrite its values, vision or mission right now. Blurred vision at the top of the organization affects your everyday ability to lead your team, but there's not very much you can do about it, is there? At this stage in your career you probably feel you lack the influence to get the organization to think about these issues right now. Of course, I would say that you have more influence than you think, and it is worth asking some questions about the vision, the mission and the values in order to establish whether they are working for the company or whether they have become an irrelevancy. You never know. Someone might listen to you.

However, for now, let's assume that you have done this and discovered that the CEO is passionate about the current, flawed Company Vision or believes values and mission are unnecessary when there is so much fire-fighting to be done.

Where does this leave you?

Make the vision relevant to you

Your company may have a vision but it seems irrelevant to the work you and your people do every day. In this case, one option is to interpret the vision in relation to what it means for the work you do in your department. Let's take Sony's vision from the 1950s. If your company vision states, "Fifty years from now, our brand name will be as well known as any in the world" but you run the IT helpdesk which fixes computer problems on site, you don't directly impact the brand name on a daily basis. How can your team be motivated by this vision?

And what about values? Sony's 1950s values included "encouraging individual ability and creativity" and "being a pioneer". And its purpose was "to experience the sheer joy of innovation and the application of technology for the benefit and pleasure of the general public".

How do you make this really resonate with your people and provide the guiding light needed?

Ask, firstly, who are the people who are directly working towards this vision on a daily basis. In this case, who will make the brand one of the best known in the world? The answer may be the marketing people or the sales team or the people in R&D.

Secondly, ask what you do for them. What does your existence enable them to do? If you are unsure, you could ask them. What would be the impact of continual IT problems on their ability to make the brand as well known as any in the world?

The obvious answer is that the IT department enables the other departments to work smoothly. Smooth running of every department means the obstacles to achieving the vision are removed. The IT department needs to be able to anticipate the needs of the other departments and respond to IT problems swiftly, so that the rest of the business can drive towards the vision without impediment. You may also get some less-obvious answers too. A smooth-running IT department may inspire the R&D people to create the next generation of technologies. Or the IT department may be the perfect test audience for new ideas.

Based on the answers you get by asking relevant stakeholders and having discussions within your own team, you may decide your vision is: "We will anticipate the needs of our colleagues and resolve IT problems with a sense of immediacy and pride, and be a fundamental lynchpin in our organization's quest to be a brand as well known as any in the world".

Now look at the values. "Being a pioneer" fits rather well with this vision for IT, but what does it really mean? Maybe the core value your department needs to focus on is "Nothing is impossible" or "No obstacle is too great". What does a pioneer believe that enables him or her to achieve the vision?

Next, look at the company purpose, which includes the words "joy" and "pleasure". Well, you can take huge joy and pleasure in what the company produces as a result of your support of the other departments. And this might be sufficient to motivate and keep you focused. Alternatively, you could identify a purpose which more closely fits your part in the overall company vision.

Your purpose may be, "To clear the path standing between our company's past and its future as a brand leader". Or it could be, "To be the right hand of every department in this organization". Consider what your "reason for being" is. What would you like your "reason for being" to be? What would you like other departments to say about your role in the business? Do you want them to say, "They fix computers"? Or do you want them to say, "They are like our right arm. We couldn't innovate without their partnership"?

In the 1950s and 1960s, everyone who worked for NASA in the USA knew what part they played in the organization's mission. If the janitor was asked what he did for a living, he would say he was putting a man on the moon. If you can make the vision, mission and values resonate with your people, or rewrite them to spell out what your team does and how it contributes to the whole, you can bring meaning to even a bland company Vision Statement.

What if the company doesn't have a vision?

This is unusual in large companies, but not so unusual in smaller businesses. Even in large companies, the vision may be a purely paper exercise and have little meaning. In the example above, the Sony vision was ambitious and invigorating. The trick was to make it relevant to your team. But where there is no vision at all you have little or nothing to build on, so you need to start from scratch.

Here is how I usually structure a workshop to identify a team vision.

1. Start by imagining that your team is firing on all cylinders, the best performing team in the company, the most admired, the most in demand. How would you describe what the team had become if that were the reality?

I encourage team members to get the colouring pens out and start drawing what their ideal future team would look like, feel like, be like on a piece of flipchart paper. Pictures that show smiley faces, sunny skies, people holding hands, light bulbs coming out of people's heads, piles of twenty pound notes and arrows all pointing in the same direction are far more honest and illustrative of what people really want. Each team member does their own picture and shares what they have drawn with their colleagues. You should do this too.

2. Then ask the team to draw what the team feels like now. You are likely to see cloudy skies, frowning faces, scribbles which signify confusion, a clock signifying long hours. Again, do the exercise yourself too. I might ask them to give the team a score out of 10 too and write that on their second picture. By this I mean, if the first picture illustrates what 10/10 would look and feel like, what score would you give the team now? This is very useful because it shows how far away from the ideal people think they are.

This whole exercise may be uncomfortable. Many people are resistant to a creative exercise like this. They ask "Draw the ideal 10/10 team? Draw where we are now? What do you mean?"

Just encourage them to do their best. The result is that people often express in pictures things they wouldn't want to express in words – their emotions, their ambitions, their fears, their honest view of the situation. There should be no judgement about the pictures. They are just a reflection of someone's feelings and opinions. At this point it is important to be open-minded about what you hear, even if it feels like your team are attacking you.

Chances are there will be some common themes emerging in both the pictures. As a team, identify what these are and make a list.

3. Once you have pictures of the current reality and the ideal, consider what values would take you to your ideal 10/10

team? What would you need to stand for? What morals would inform your decisions and your behaviour?

Dig deep here. Write down the obvious ones related to honesty and high quality. But get the thesaurus out and look for more precise words to describe what you really mean. You can explain that some of the obvious values are "entry level". But what higher standard would we need to hold ourselves to in order to really achieve this ideal picture? The Disney Corporation has "creativity, dreams and imagination"[7] amongst its values (as you might expect). Harley Davidson has "Keep your promises" rather than honesty and integrity. Intel wants to "Communicate mutual intentions and expectations" as a way to form partnerships with their customers and suppliers.[8] If your values say what you really mean rather than being meaningless because they are so bland, your people are more likely to remember them and to hold one another to that standard every day.

4. Now you can consider purpose – your reason for being. Without a company vision you may not be very clear about what the organization you work for is trying to achieve. But you can still strive to have a reason for being within that organization. Why is it important you exist? And why is that important? And why is that important? Keep asking until you get to the root of your purpose or mission.

Remember not just to describe what you do but what you achieve by doing it and for whom. So, Mary Kay Cosmetics say their purpose is "To give unlimited opportunity to women". Nike say "To experience the emotion of competition, winning and crushing competitors". At Disney it is "To make people happy" and at Wal-Mart "To give ordinary folk the chance to buy the same things as rich people".[9]

When you and your team read your purpose, it should make you smile, make you feel determined and make what you do every day feel worthy. If you feel what you do has no value and no worth, it is not going to inspire you every day. If you see how your daily toil impacts other people, the organization or even the planet, you can feel pride in what you do.

Now you need to add some flavour.

5. This is where a big bold goal and a bit of creative writing come in. Your big team goal doesn't have to have a number attached, but it does need to be measurable. So you could say, "A computer in every household in America" (Microsoft's early goal) or, "To become a $125 billion company by the year 2000" (Wal-Mart in the 1990s), which are measurable numbers. Or you could be as provocative and measurable without a number, like Nike in the 1960s "Crush Adidas" or "Become the Harvard of the West" (Stanford University in the 1940s).

This big goal should be bold, it should seem beyond reach within the next 10–30 years (but it should be reachable), and it should create butterflies in your stomach. As a department your goal may be "To attract 200 top-class applicants for every job vacancy" or "To be top in our company engagement survey every year between now and 2030" or "To set the benchmark in our field for efficiency, innovation and quality".

6. Alongside this you need a vivid description of what gold at the finishing line would look like. Look at all those pictures you drew to describe 10/10. What were the themes? Did everyone want to build a team that was a pleasure to be part of? Did people want to be appreciated for their contribution? Did they want other teams to ask, "What's your secret?" Build this into a vivid description. Think of it as a rallying call. A call to arms.

If you like, write it in the future tense, using "We will be …" rather than "We are …" This will encourage you to be bolder because it is clearly an aspiration rather than a description of the situation as it is now.

Going back to the Sony example from the 1950s, Sony said "We will create products that become persuasive around the world … We will be the first Japanese company to go into the US market and distribute directly … [our brand name] will signify innovation and quality that rival the most innovative companies anywhere …" It is a list of ambitions which must, at the time, have seemed ridiculous. Your vivid description should make you all feel a bit scared too. You should wonder if you have aimed too high or been too dramatic.

TEAM VISION AND THE ART OF COMMUNICATION

Having a team vision is one thing. But you must also be dedicated to communicating it. We have seen what can happen if people are left with more questions than answers. They fill the void with guess work and gossip.

It can be hugely frustrating as a leader-manager to have a clear vision and to have talked about it endlessly with your people and still hear feedback like "I don't know where we are going" and "I think we need more direction".

The leader-managers I have worked with who have this problem sometimes feel like they are alone, a voice in the wilderness, which other people in the business are either wilfully ignoring or too stupid to comprehend.

Unfortunately, saying something over and over isn't the same thing as communicating. And communicating well isn't a step-by-step process. It is like every part of being a manager or a leader, a continual journey where you make small (and large) adjustments continually in order to chart a relatively straight course.

Listen

Communication doesn't start with speaking. It starts with listening. You want to know how people feel, what is really going on in your team and what obstacles there are to turning the team vision into reality. There are a number of sources of information and a number of different ways to listen, but here are a few.

1. Listen to your trusted advisors – these are not necessarily your peers (although they might be). They may be from inside the

business or outside. They are people who generally give you good counsel and who don't have a huge vested interest in the outcome. No matter how neutral people believe they are being, they usually have a bias. If someone is going to be directly impacted by a change you are proposing, they will, unconsciously or consciously, give a biased response. If you don't feel you have trusted advisors, consider how you could begin to build this kind of network. Ask these trusted advisors what obstacles they perceive. Ask them to challenge you hard about your vision and values. Tell them the vision and see if they get it. And, of course, ask them if they have heard rumours or gossip which suggest there are gaps in understanding of your true intentions.

2. Listen to "positive deviants"[10] – these are the people in your business who are already doing things in a radically better way. They may be seen as trouble-makers because they do their own thing. They may be the best performers in the company (or in your team). They are not necessarily popular. But they are very interesting because they look at problems and solutions in different ways to the majority. They will give you a fresh perspective on your vision. They may help you upgrade it and become more ambitious. They may tell you which aspects of the vision have significance for them and which don't. And they may tell you whether you are walking the talk or not.

3. Listen to the grassroots – you might think the receptionist, the cleaner, the office administrator or the telesales office don't know much about the business and care even less. However, they see how the decisions made at the top of the organization

translate in real life. They deal with the fallout. And they often have different sources of information from you. You may have heard the MD speak about the company vision in person. Your team may have heard your spin on the company vision. But the receptionist heard about all of that via email from her friend in Accounts. The information she has tells you a lot about how messages are received and how they are interpreted.

4. Listen to customers – it can be intimidating to ask customers (whether internal or external) for feedback or for opinions. Some managers worry they will be so overwhelmed by ideas, criticisms and opinions that they prefer not to know. This is clearly a dangerous approach, meaning all of those ideas, criticisms and opinions are still out there. You just don't know about them. Ignorance is not bliss. But if you are willing to hear what customers are telling you (even if you decide not to act on a lot of what you hear), you will at least be informed and able to make educated decisions in future.

5. Listen to yourself – you probably have inklings. That voice in your head which acts as an early warning system for you should be heard. You are not going to act on it in isolation because you are also listening to other sources of information. But when you trust your gut you can at least take responsibility for your actions and for their results. If on occasion you turn out to be wrong, learn from that and "educate" your intuition. But it is much easier to live with your mistakes when you know they were truly yours. If you suspect your message is not getting through, don't ignore these feelings. Find new ways to communicate the same message and eventually you may be

able to pull your whole team together, all facing in the same direction.

Listening is important at all stages when creating a company or team vision. It will give you a sense of whether your people know what the vision is. It will show you to what extent that vision provides a useful compass. It will show you what is preventing that vision from being understood and "owned" by the staff. And it will give you clues as to what that vision would need to be if it were to come to life within the business.

Listen to the uncomfortable truths you are being told, even if they seen like criticisms of you. If people are willing to share that with you, you know you have created some sort of trust. Take it as good news and keep an open mind. You had the courage to recognize that something wasn't right and you took the brave step to ask about it. Don't be surprised that other people have been feeling the same way and that they think you are part of the problem.

Ask the right questions

One of the causes of the blame culture is over-reliance on the question "Why?" I don't suggest we ban questions beginning with "Why?", but I do think the word "Why" needs to be better understood before it is used.

Firstly, "Why" is hard to say in a neutral tone of voice. It just sounds accusatory. The only way to stop it sounding like that is to take all the emotion out of your voice and try not to emphasize any words. And then what you end up with is a question which has no passion and makes you sound like a robot.

Secondly, "Why" tends to get a negative response. The first reply you will get is probably "I don't know", which is a natural response to the question but sets a tone. When someone says "I don't know" they can seem obstructive or just ignorant. In reality, they probably do know but the question isn't a great tool for accessing the answer.

I believe questions beginning with "What" and "How" are under-utilised. "What" and "How" questions tend to access more fruitful responses. You could ask someone, "Why did that happen?" Alternatively, you could ask "What happened? What caused that to happen? How did everyone react?"

You may think there is little difference. In fact, the difference is significant. These "What?" questions will provide you with some facts. They sound neutral. And, in order to ask questions beginning with "What?" authentically you must also assume a neutral frame of mind, otherwise this is just a technique. Instead of the shirking of responsibility and the passing on of blame that you get when you ask "Why did that happen?", you get an account of events where people have the opportunity to take responsibility for their part in that story.

"What" and "How" questions don't only provide you with facts. They also help you get to the root cause of problems, i.e. "What is the common denominator here?", "What are we learning?" and "What is the root cause of the problem?"

They also help you think of solutions, i.e. "What could we do differently?", "What ideas do we have?" and "What could turn this situation to our favour?"

And they also help you make decisions, i.e. "What is the best course of action now?", "How are we going to respond?" and "How do we make sure this decision sticks?"

"What" and "How" questions are "open" rather than closed in that they can be answered with more than just a yes or no. So they are great for encouraging participation and getting a debate going.

When it comes to establishing a vision, the ability to ask these kinds of questions is key. You need people to think about what is working well and what isn't. You need them to imagine what 10/10 looks like or what the ideal working environment would be. You need them to tell you what their values are and what values would enable the team to achieve its big goal. All of these questions begin with "What" and "How".

So, if you have a vision but fear it hasn't been fully understood, you could just repeat it again. Or you could ask people, "What would you want the vision to be? What problems would you like the vision to address? How would you like your colleagues and me to behave?" Then show them how the vision you created describes the future they have just been asking for. They have just told you they want their colleagues to be honest and right here, at the bottom of page one of your Team Vision, it clearly states "We will speak straight. We will tell it how it is".

And, of course, you can ask "What does this vision mean for you? What difference would you be able to make if you lived by these values? What do you need from me?"

Out of that conversation may come some clear actions for you or your team to take. Now they can see what they are doing and, ironically, why (without you ever asking a "Why" question or explaining "why" in so many words). "What" and "How" allow people to walk through the vision at their own pace and see how it is relevant and meaningful for them. They join the dots so you don't have to do it for them.

Communicating by listening and asking questions rather than telling may seem time-consuming. But it is far less time-consuming than repeating the same mantra over and over knowing it remains meaningless and irrelevant to most people.

Asking questions also helps you understand what your senior managers expect of you and why. Questions help you bring meaning to the company vision and prevent you wasting time on activities which are not core to the vision of the organization.

John Barnes remembers when he was a junior manager who knew little of his company's vision and purpose. He says that asking the right questions helped him to understand what the company was driving towards and how he could be part of that:

"When I was a more junior manager I would worry about how quickly I could get something done or the quality I could put in to my work to impress someone. Now I realize I have to understand more about exactly why someone needs something doing because quite often the running around and doing stuff gets a different outcome than the one which was intended. So now I try to unpack the initial requirements to understand what the motivation is. Instead of responding to the instruction 'Go and do such and such' I get something of the problem as well as the solution. If I had done this early in my career I would have wasted a lot less time doing things that weren't really what was intended. And I would have learned more quickly about what the level above me is seeing in terms of the bigger picture."

Asking questions may seem like an innate skill, or certainly one we should have picked up during our formal education. But, John Barnes says, the education system doesn't reflect the realities of working in business. In fact, it conditions us not to question:

"The education system gives you homework. Do these sums, write this poem or answer this question. It doesn't tell you why you are doing it. So you get into the world of work and you are asked for this report and these figures and you think 'Oh, this is like school. I know how to do that', so off you trot and do it. In fact, the world of work would be a more interesting place if you asked these questions, particularly at the beginning of your career when you've got a lot of just 'doing' activity."

Communicate to different populations

Effective communicators adjust their message to appeal to their audience. This doesn't mean they promise conflicting rewards to different people, or lie just to placate a certain part of the business. But they find what is true and will also have meaning for each person or each constituency they need to win.

One way to do this is to create what John Kotter calls a "powerful guiding coalition".[11] This means you are not the only one speaking but are backed up by a group of leaders or opinion-formers who influence attitudes in your part of the business. That way, when it comes to talking about the vision, or the purpose or the values of your team, you are not an isolated voice but one of many people calling the team to action. When a whole organization is changing direction or re-visioning its future, Kotter says it takes not only the chair or president or divisional manager to be supportive of the change but also another 5–15 people (even 50 people) to "come together and develop a shared commitment to excellent performance through renewal".[12]

As you go about listening to the various information holders in the business and asking the right questions, you will begin to recognize who might be part of this guiding coalition ... and who will not. Not everyone is going to buy in, especially at first, so you may want to draw in people who are not necessarily the most senior but who are advocates for what you are trying to achieve.

This can mean you ruffle some feathers. Some colleagues are going to feel left out. But this is inevitable. If the hierarchy was working well there would be no need for change.

Another way to speak to different populations is through the use of "story". Stories can reinforce your company or team values. They become part of the mythology of the workplace.

There are far too few of the right kinds of stories in business. The stories we normally hear are those that come from the rumour machine, stories about someone who spoke up in a meeting and was fired the next day, someone who tried to solve a customer complaint by taking matters into their own hands and was hauled before the company lawyer, someone who came up with a great idea but was ridiculed by their manager.

If you want to make your vision, mission and values live, you will benefit from having stories to tell about colleagues who have demonstrated it in real life. And in telling this story, you have to be "real" yourself. You have to give credit to someone else (the story probably won't be about how brilliant you are but how brilliant someone else is), and show your true feelings. Jim Sinegal, the cofounder and CEO of Costco, the American retail chain, recounts a story which has become myth in that business. At the time the company was making a great deal of money from selling Calvin Klein jeans at $29.99 each. Then, one of their buyers managed to buy a new batch of the jeans which could be sold at $22.99 with the same profit margin for Costco. Costco could have kept charging their customers $29.99 and pocketed the extra $7. After all, no customer was going to know that this batch was cheaper than the last. But instead, they passed the cost saving on and cut the price of the jeans. Costco's culture dictates that their success is due to their focus on customers getting value for money. In that context there was nothing else they could have done.[13]

It is also important that you tell stories that have importance to those you are talking to. The same story as told to the Buying Department at Costco will be different when told to the Store Managers. You want to make heroes of the people you are talking to. You don't want the Store Managers to feel they are hearing all about how brilliant the Buyers are, as if Store Managers have nothing to do with the success of the business. In order to do this well, you will need to prepare. Even the most natural of storytellers practices their story and tests it, refining it as they go.

Being a storyteller isn't how you make your living, but it is part of being a leader-manager. You want these stories about the vision, the mission and the values to be as powerful as the stories which emerge from the rumour machine. Those stories are full of good guys and bad guys, intrigue and mystery, plot twists and surprise endings. And they are always made relevant to the audience. You need your stories to be even greater blockbusters.

TURNING VISION INTO ACTION

Of course, a vision has no value if it remains disconnected from everyday work. You may now have helped your people to see the connection between the company vision and the vision of the team. And, if they understand your priorities in relation to that vision, they will be able to prioritize more effectively themselves. But a vision should be able to do more than that. It should translate into real plans which overcome real obstacles and get real results.

It's a problem Karen Mellor has noticed in her company's vision:

"The overall company vision is pretty well known. The tricky bit is knowing what your contribution to the overall vision is. I find that is less well known. People interpret what they think it means. There has to be an opportunity for people to focus on their passions and this desire should be nurtured where you are working in an innovation based industry. However their interpretation of the vision may not be shared by everyone in the organization and this is where it goes wrong – with too many unstructured innovative projects or activities and with little transparency and structure. The vision really is to be 'one' pharmaceutical company all pulling together rather than different parts of the organization following different interpretations."

To overcome this, especially if you have developed a vision for the team, you will go back to your vision, mission and values and use them as a starting point. Consider what they mean in terms of:

- Areas of focus – what is your core work?
- Measurable goals – in addition to the ultimate goal, what other shorter-term goals do you need to set?
- The limits of what you do – be clear on what you don't do, as well as what you do.

Now, when you are clear on this, break it down still further into "how". What are the programmes you run or the projects you are involved in? What projects and programmes would you need to be involved in (that you can anticipate now) in order to achieve the vision? What are you not doing that you ought to be doing as a team or organization? What obstacles do you foresee and how are you going to overcome them?

This part of the plan enables you to be proactive. Instead of juggling projects handed to you by your line managers or by "fate", you are getting very clear about what your efforts *should* be put into.

When you compare this strategy with the ways you currently spend time, there should be a discrepancy. If you cannot find one you have either set too low a target or you are not being honest with each other about how you spend your time.

This creates an opportunity to stop doing certain kinds of work, as well as clarity about what you should be doing. Now it all comes down to your relationship with your line management. If you are clearer about where your focus should be and have identified where your time should be spent, in order to achieve the vision and aid the company in winning gold, you will need your line managers to buy-in and give you permission to make the changes you believe are necessary.

NATURAL RESISTANCE TO CHANGE

A powerful, compelling vision should inspire people to change how they do things, what they do and why. It should provide focus and context. It should also set the tone through clarifying values and, out of it, a clear set of priorities should flow. From there work, and the way work is completed, should start to feel and be different. Not everyone likes it when things change.

We each have a different attitude towards change. Some of us are quite risk-averse and we like what we know. When change is thrust upon us we feel negative emotions about how this change is going to impact us, our ability to adapt to the change and how different everything is going to be as a result. People like this have a preference for things staying the same. Try not to judge them. There will probably have been times when you displayed this preference; for instance, at the end of a relationship, if you've ever been made redundant or if the local authority gave permission for a superstore at the end of your garden. In the end, you may have found that the change was better than you expected, led to something even greater than what you lost or that you surprised yourself by how well you coped. But before, when the change was just a proposal, you probably experienced some negativity, simply because it was going to be a change.

Then there are people who predominantly want things to be the same but they enjoy the prospect of some change. They don't mind a bit of change but they want to know some things are going to stay the same. This is the person who is happy to be moving house but still wants to go to the same hairdresser and the same café after the move. This is the person who is pleased to be getting a promotion but still wants to be invited for lunch by her un-promoted friends. This is the person who is glad the football club built a new stadium but wants to sit in the same position behind the goal that he has always sat in.

A friend of mine once told me, when I had changed my career and my personal situation and swapped life in the city for life in the countryside, that it is called a "comfort zone" for a reason. His view was that there was nothing innately wrong about spending some time in my comfort zone. It wasn't necessary to disrupt all elements of my life simultaneously. Consider if there have been times in your life when everything – home, personal, family, work, leisure, financial, health – was up in the air. It is very uncomfortable for most people when nothing is stable. Most of us find we can cope with a certain amount of disruption if other aspects of life are constant. To a certain extent we all have (more or less) a "same, but different" attitude to change. When your colleagues resist change, ask yourself how much other disruption they are experiencing in their life. They may be finding this particular change harder than usual because it coincides with other changes in their life.

The final group of people love when things change. They thrive on it. In fact, they may even cause problems in order to find solutions and new ways of doing things. They get bored with life if today is like yesterday. It is stability not change which worries them. These are the people who take up new hobbies every six months. These are the people who move jobs regularly. These are the people who would never holiday in the same place twice or order their "favourites" when shopping online.

Whilst you may believe that this approach to change is the most useful, it has problems of its own. These people get quite frustrated by the pace of change, which tends to be slow. They find it hard to appreciate that other people, who prefer a slower pace, need to be listened to and adapted to. As a manager, your ease with change may prevent you being as empathetic with members of your team as your need to be.

And, when things settle down at the end of a phase of dramatic change, you may feel a bit lost. What gets you up in the morning when everything at work is just ticking along?

When communicating change, you need to consider your whole audience. Tell people what is going to be the same first. Then tell them what is going to be a little bit different. And then tell them what is going to be completely different. Finally, if you feel you need to, talk again about what is going to be the same. As with any form of communication, you will need to keep repeating the message and demonstrating what you mean through your actions. You will need to reward the sort of behaviour you want to see and correct the sort of behaviour you don't. And you will need to keep doing this until the change phase is over.

BLURRED VISION – FINAL THOUGHTS

Karen Mellor reminded me of the part in *Alice in Wonderland* where Alice asks the Cheshire cat which way to go.

Alice: Would you tell me, please, which way I ought to go from here?
The Cat: That depends a good deal on where you want to get to.
Alice: I don't much care where.
The Cat: Then it doesn't much matter which way you go.

Having a vision is like that. You are certainly busy. No one can argue with that. But where are you going? If you don't know where you want to get to, it doesn't much matter what you do every day.

And that is the point. If people don't think it matters much what they do all day, you will experience serious problems of motivation, loyalty, engagement, creativity and everything else that makes for a great workplace.

You don't have to transform your whole organization to have a vision. You can just change the lives of the people who work with you directly. When people arrive at work every day clear about what is really important about what they do and how their work plays a part in the success of the whole operation, many of those petty problems which zap your time and energy and prevent you being the kind of manager you want to be, just disappear. And most of the remaining problems get resolved by members of the team and never land on your desk. A route map provides people at all levels in an organization with context for what they do and enables them to make wise decisions without having to seek your approval every time. That makes a massive difference to your life for certain.

It means you can really step back from the day-to-day operations occasionally and think, plan, read, ponder, innovate, learn and enjoy what you do. Wouldn't that make a big enough difference to you (and to your team) to make work feel like it worked much better?

In your newly discovered thinking and planning time you may decide to tackle one of the greatest obstacles to a happy working life – the fact that companies do not work as single entities. They are more like kingdoms with warring clans. Yes, it is the dreaded silo mentality that we need to look at next.

Frustration 4: Silo Mentality

"But why should I help the Chiswick branch when I am rewarded for the results I achieve at the Hammersmith branch?"

It was a question that took me by surprise. We had been working together for a day and a half at a lovely training facility in the Kent countryside. The atmosphere at the team-building workshop had been cordial and we had all enjoyed good food and fine wine together the previous evening. All the delegates had thrown themselves into exercises with their colleagues, all of whom were branch managers for one of the major high-street banks.

Just before the surprising question, I had been suggesting that one of the many benefits of branch managers working as a team would be that the whole region would perform better. If more successful branches shared their expertise with less successful branches that would benefit the bank as a whole, and therefore those branch managers who helped poorer performing branches would stand out as high potential promotion prospects. Surely.

What I hadn't fully understood was that each branch's performance was measured against other branches of their own bank. If Chiswick started getting better results, Hammersmith's results would look poorer by comparison. Bonuses were based on where your branch stood in a league table of branches of your own bank, not how your branch was faring in comparison with competitor banks.

I quickly realized that branches were not rewarded for supporting one another. They were rewarded for outperforming one another. The whole concept of branch managers working as a team of peers was fundamentally undermined by a bonus system that forced them to view one another as competitors, not colleagues.

It is a phenomenon I see regularly. Organizations which are set up to sustain factions, create competition between different parts of their own business and prevent information being available to everyone.

When companies operate like this, we describe these isolated parts of the same business as "silos". And silos are one of the greatest frustrations of the people I work with. They are also bad for business.

A company is like a living organism, all of its parts are interconnected. The brain requires blood, which is pumped by the heart. The heart is kept healthy when we move our bodies a bit. By moving our legs and arms we stay fit, which is good for the heart. When we feel fit we feel happy. So, emotions and physical fitness and mental activity are all interrelated at all times. If the heart can't pump blood into the brain or the body stops moving or the brain switches off, the rest of the body cannot function properly.

It is just like that in a business. When marketing and sales don't talk, or when IT isn't consulted about the introduction of a new accounting process or when there is friction between HR and Finance, parts of the organization become starved of blood. When looked at in isolation they seem fine – people are busy, they are having meetings, they are processing their work, clearing their inbox. But they are not contributing to the rest of the organization. They are cut off.

If your company is highly "siloed", you will constantly feel that you are swimming against the tide whenever you try to seek information, work on projects with other parts of the business or find out why something went wrong. Still unsure whether silos are a problem in your organization? Here are some other symptoms of "silo mentality":

- Information is not readily available. You ask a question of someone outside your immediate team and the response is slow, irrelevant or non-existent.
- You don't know people in other parts of the business. You may have spoken to one or two on the phone, or exchanged emails, but your friendships and core working relationships are mainly within your own team or function.
- You don't know how your work contributes to the success of the business. You know what your team targets are and how you are progressing against those targets, but you don't know how that impacts the rest of the business.
- There is animosity (even distrust and possibly hatred) between your team and other teams.
- You are encouraged to focus on your competition inside the business not your competition outside the business. Maybe you aren't even told who your competitors outside the business are.
- You are not rewarded for adding value to other parts of the organization, only for adding value to your part of the organization.
- You don't know what other parts of the organization do.
- You don't know who to go to when there is a problem.
- When you do go to other parts of the business with a problem there are numerous hoops to jump through, red-tape to negotiate and personality issues to overcome which make solving the problem together difficult.

- You are physically separated from other parts of your company. People don't visit other parts of the company, even if they are down one flight of stairs or across a busy street.
- Ideas are not shared, so you feel you are constantly reinventing the wheel even though you suspect other parts of your company must have the same problems and may have developed some good solutions.
- Your team or function works in a very different way, with different processes, technology, administration, structure and culture to the rest of the business. When you do try to work with colleagues in other parts of the business you find you are incompatible.
- The top team do not get on.

You probably don't experience all of these symptoms. I hope not. But some will probably be familiar. And what makes silos all the more frustrating is that you can clearly see the lost opportunity cost of working in this way.

WHY SILOS WORK

Of course, companies wouldn't create a siloed culture if it didn't work at some level. There are some very good reasons why companies are structured in this way and why silos are overlooked.

Power – A certain personality seeks power. People like this, who have spent 10, 20 or 30 years working their way up the career ladder, want to have something to show for it. All the time they are kowtowing to the boss, going along with policies they disagree with, keeping their nose to the grindstone and being a good company employee, they are waiting for the day when they are senior enough to preside over other lesser mortals. In order to have that reassuring feeling that they have "made it", they need a patch to call their own. In very flat organizations or cross-functional organizations, territory is not so easy to define and that feeling of being in charge is diluted.

I have been rather harsh. It is easy to look at your line manager or your manager's manager and say "Look at that power-hungry tyrant". Not all leaders are like this, and many want to break up the silos as much as you do. But, in truth, most of us like having some authority and influence and we are reluctant to give much of it up.

Efficiency – Companies are structured to be efficient. That's why re-structures are quite common. Those at the top want to ensure the way they organize their people and the functions within the business make the most sense. There is a belief that if you get the structure right, work will flow more easily. This takes us back to that idea of a business as a machine with working parts. Keep all the parts in good working order and the business will tick over. But this never-ending search for the perfect structure is a distraction in my view because businesses (and the people in them) operate less like machines and more like living organisms. What is far more important is that different parts of the business talk to each other and that boundaries between different territories are broken down. But the desire to get efficiency lies behind the creation of highly structured organizations and excessive structure can lead to silos.

Competition – There is a belief that a bit of healthy competition between teams is good for productivity. If two branches of the same bank are trying to get to the top of the league table they will work much harder than they might otherwise do in order to win. This is meant to be fun. It is meant to create a high bar to aim for which keeps everyone focused on doing better, making more sales, cutting costs, improving the bottom line. The intention is, again, positive.

Lack of breadth – When people become knowledgeable they are reluctant to become novices again. If you are performing very well in your little niche in the business and you are recognized and rewarded for that, there is very little incentive to step out of that comfort zone and be a beginner again. I remember hearing the chef, Gordon Ramsay, speaking at a business event explaining why he changed restaurants so many times early in his career. In each place he would learn all the basics again. Each chef he worked for had a specific style and method and Ramsay would have to learn that style and method, even though it was different from the style and method he had been taught by his previous head chef. He could have stayed put once he learnt what would satisfy his boss and just kept making soufflé or soup that way. Instead, he went back to square one in each new job. The benefit, of course, was that he learnt far more variety and eventually was able to draw on all of that knowledge to develop his own unique style and method. And, because he was equally familiar with different styles and different parts of the kitchen, he could see how they were all interconnected – how a problem in one part of the kitchen impacted another part of the kitchen, how success in one part of the kitchen could help another part improve its quality too.

By contrast, leaders in business tend to have expertise in quite narrow areas. They don't work in different parts of the business early in their career, but specialize. This lack of breadth prevents them seeing opportunities for cross-functional working, identifying common ground between different parts of the business and having the confidence to build relationships outside their own area.

Speed – When you work in a silo you don't have to consult other parts of the organization before you act. This means you can respond far quicker to problems and develop solutions which work perfectly for your part of the business. If other parts of the business are facing similar problems they can resolve them, or not. If you believe your responsibility is only to make your team or function work as well as it can, you will find the delays involved in getting a cross-functional team together time-consuming and expensive. Small units are quicker than large units.

The speed of silo working is an argument which Karen Mellor hears often in her job. She is working on a global approach to problem solving in her company but finds individual managers want to press on with their own, local solutions:

"I was meant to bring in a company-wide resource management system. Only last week a manager said he was going to introduce resource management himself for his area of the business. When challenged and told every area needed this he said, 'But I need it now'. But we all need it now. Some leaders have this concept of going it alone. But what is the point in them using their resources to create something that the whole organization needs? The attitude is 'I need it now. I am going to do it and hope others think it is a good idea and they take it on'. And when they have put their effort into creating something they are very reluctant to let it go. So when we try to harmonize across the business people don't want to change their way of doing things."

THE LOST OPPORTUNITY

There are some powerful reasons why silos exist. But what is the cost to you and your organization of silos? Apart from being frustrating, are you paying a more tangible price?

Information – Your business is filled with experts. No matter how junior or how senior you and your colleagues are, you all bring to your work a lifetime of experiences, education, training, ideas and talents. If it were possible to release all of that untapped energy into your business, you can imagine how much more valuable that business would be. If ideas, information, learning and expertise flowed with ease around the organization, the whole entity could move forward more quickly. However, when there are barriers to that information being shared it remains locked in certain parts of the business. Although perceived as quicker, siloed organizations are slower because people can't access the information or expertise they need.

Creativity – When two seemingly unrelated concepts collide, ideas are born. When two parts of a business get together and start talking, they develop ideas which neither part of the business could have generated in isolation. Back in the 1970s the electric toothbrush was making a big splash in the electronics market. They were all the rage. But despite the Gillette Group including Braun (which makes small electrical appliances), Duracell (which makes batteries) and Oral B (which makes toothbrushes), it lost out to its competitors who got to market first with a popular electric toothbrush. Because Braun, Duracell and Oral B didn't talk to each other, despite being part of the same group, they didn't realize they had all the experience to develop a successful electric toothbrush until they noticed their competitors doing it.

Focus internally instead of externally – Companies with silo problems tend to be inward looking. This means they don't spend enough time or place enough importance on analysing threats which come from outside the business. What matters is not how you compare with another part of the business but how you, as a business, are doing in relation to your competitors. It is your competitors who will put you out of business, take your best clients and put you under financial pressure, not your colleagues.

Paul Currah has been aware of silos in nearly every company he has worked in. He says it takes a brave person to question the status quo:

"You need to have the courage to say 'What are we really here for?' I am sure I propped the silos up occasionally. Some of the stuff I had to do in my last job was about filling in stuff online, spreadsheets or something that provided data and information for people so the department could demonstrate its contribution. That in itself creates a level of work where people go off to find evidence to prove how effective that department is being. That is, of itself, unproductive and not adding value to the whole organization but doing PR for a department within an organization. It is desperately sad when departments feel the need to do their own PR."

Problems are hidden – Silos are great at protecting poor performers and unethical behaviour. It is possible to operate under the radar, to keep a low profile and hide your behaviour from the rest of the business. Often, when unprofessional activities are revealed, the vast majority of people working in the rest of the organization can honestly claim that they had no idea such behaviour was going on. Some of the recent high-profile ethical failures in companies like Enron have been blamed on silos. They are bad for transparency and mean that people who do not have the best interests of the business at heart can get away with activity which is detrimental to the organization and remain undiscovered for years.

Silos are career limiting – If your only experience of your industry is within your small part of your business, your value as you move up the hierarchy is limited. You don't have operational experience or you lack practical skills, or you don't do numbers or you aren't experienced internationally, or you aren't commercial or you don't have a broad perspective, or you can't see past the shop floor ... I have seen many highly talented managers hit a career brick wall because they have become increasingly insular, developing depth of expertise without breadth of expertise. When they try to get promoted out of their silo they are often told they are not suited to a more general management role.

Silos produce lopsided companies – Of course, some people are promoted out of their silo despite having little breadth of expertise. You often find the chief executive or managing director is fundamentally an accountant, a salesperson or a technical expert who has moved up as the organization grew or who managed to get a top job when an accountant, a salesperson or a technical expert was deemed to be required. At certain times, someone with a depth of expertise but lacking breadth is a good option. If a company needs to radically refocus on sales or needs to get its numbers in order, or wants to prioritize new product development, it will often benefit, in the short term, from a CEO who has quite a narrow focus. In general, though, the top team should be made up of people who can cast their eye across the whole company, notice trends, think globally, understand the interconnectedness of the various units in the business. When you put an accountant, a sales-person or a technical expert in the CEO's chair you end up with a lopsided business which tends to focus on the aspects of business that the individual feels comfortable with. Other important issues or opportunities are missed because they are not considered impor-tant or are not understood by the people at the top. If that lopsided individual is surrounded by people lopsided in the same direction, the company can topple over.

START WHERE YOU WILL GET THE BIGGEST RETURN

Of course, the best solution for fixing a silo problem is taking a company-wide approach. You can't break down silos one silo at a time. However, you are unlikely to have the authority to take a company-wide approach. That's the problem, isn't it? You are sitting in your silo, frustrated about the silos but unable to act because there are limited opportunities to step out of the silo and do something cross-functional.

All is not lost though.

There are probably some key relationships with other parts of the business that, if they were closer, would give you the biggest bang for your buck. An example would be the relationship between marketing and sales teams. Typically, the tension between these two teams is something like sibling rivalry. In many companies, marketing feels that sales takes all the credit for work which was largely down to good marketing. And sales sees marketing as a group of creatives who don't do the real work of closing sales. In the end though, marketing and sales should be on the same team. What is their job really about? It is about attracting and converting customers, thereby bringing money into the business. Marketing and sales are two parts of the same process. There may be a distinction in terms of the skills required, but the purpose is the same. And, in organizations where marketing and sales work together (or where there is no distinction at all), messages and approaches to the potential customer are aligned.

You could even argue that sales and marketing are pivotal to new product development too, although it is a rare R&D department which consults sales and marketing before they have developed a product. Usually they are handed the product at the end and told "sell that". But when new products are developed in isolation from sales and marketing, you often end up with products and services which look great on paper but don't meet a customer need or can't be explained in such a way as to make them appealing to potential clients. Sales people have direct knowledge of customers, marketers have in-depth knowledge of communicating messages to an audience, and product development people have a talent for converting raw ideas into real products and services. Working together, they can produce something which practically sells itself.

Cross-team working addresses far more everyday challenges too. In one organization I work with, accounts are processed by one team but cheques are signed by another. The accounts team work as efficiently as they can but are constantly held up by the team who can sign cheques. As a consequence, the accounts department spends a great deal of time answering calls from suppliers complaining about unpaid invoices but they have no authority to do anything about the situation. The team who write the cheques have other responsibilities too, cheque-writing being only one, so they cannot always prioritize this activity. When a mistake is made and an invoice is unpaid, it is always unclear where the mistake occurred and both teams have a vested interest in blaming the other. Resolving this problem by combining the teams or simply improving processes and information sharing would reduce workloads, improve supplier relationships and cut stress levels.

As consumers and members of the public, we are at the sharp end of silos too. Belinda has seen first-hand what problems silo thinking in the NHS creates when it comes to delivery of healthcare services:

"The silos make my job interesting but also ridiculous. The people in primary care trusts often haven't worked in a hospital, and the people in the hospital have no respect for the trusts because they often don't know how they work. For instance, if you have a fall you need hospital care, then some rehabilitation and then some other support from social services. But the money is split three ways into hospital, primary care and social services, so the patient has to fill in three forms to access three different services. In an ideal world an elderly patient who had a fall would just have access to everything they might need. A tension is created and everyone points their finger at someone else. They aren't often focused on solving the problem but on pointing the finger. Maybe it is because they are paranoid about being seen to do the wrong thing. The negative press is phenomenal, so lots of people in the NHS live in fear. There is a sense of competition but also deep paranoia."

GO TO THE SOURCE

There is a great deal of vested interest in silos and when you go about breaking down some of those walls between you and other parts of the organization, there are bound to be conflicts and tensions. But you need to start somewhere. Ask yourself, which silo (team, function, unit, location, manager) is creating the greatest difficulty for you and your team? Which problem, if it were resolved, would bring the greatest reward in terms of reduced workload, greater efficiency, reduced stress, clarity, focus on adding real value or harmonious relationships at work?

Chances are, if it is a problem for you it is a problem for the other team too. And, chances are as strongly as you feel it is their fault, they think it is yours.

Getting together with the people who seem to be causing the problem may be uncomfortable. Of course, if it were easy you would have done it by now. Unless you get to the root cause of the difficulties between you and another part of the business, any effort to resolve them will be piecemeal at best.

The meeting (or series of meetings, because this is unlikely to be resolved in one go) should look like the Monthly Strategic Meetings discussed in the meetings section of this book (Frustration 1). The main objective is to get all the conflicts out into the open. If you know, deep down, that you are competitive in nature (like most ambitious people) and that, at some level, the tensions between you and the other team are related to your desire to win, it is best to be honest. You may want to think in advance about how to express this clearly and accurately so as not to be misinterpreted. But your opposite number probably already knows and your honesty will set the tone. At the same time, talk about the positives – your respect for your opposite number, or your appreciation for their expertise, or your liking of them on a human level (but make sure the positives are true for you).

Encourage everyone present to list the problems they experience and how they feel before you start exploring options for solving the problems or debating who is right and who is wrong.

Once you feel there are no more elephants in the room, you can take the problems in turn (or choose one that feels most fundamental) and start talking about what the ideal solution might look and feel like. Don't worry about the detail, just find areas of common ground. What would you be capable of together if you overcame this problem? If the problems were overcome, what would be the benefits?

There may be agreement that overcoming these problems would make both teams more efficient. There may be agreement that overcoming these problems would enhance the customer service of both teams. There may be agreement that overcoming these problems would make everyone involved look good and improve their chances of a bonus.

What you are looking for as you start to agree areas of common purpose is a single project you can work on together to enhance your relationship and demonstrate the value of working in a more cross-functional manner. It is what Patrick Lencioni calls a Thematic Goal.[1] A thematic goal is a single focus that is shared by a group but that applies for only a specific time period. You aren't trying to create a joint vision. It isn't as big as that. You are trying to identify a shared top priority which requires you to do something together within a relatively short period of time. The "doing something together" bit is vital, because you can have vague discussions about shared priorities and find nothing really changes unless you have agreed to take action.

In establishing what this Thematic Goal might be, get as many ideas as possible from your colleagues. You want people to share their most unrealistic, outlandish, unworkable, expensive, cheap, long-term, short-term, silly, obvious, flawed ideas (as well as their simple, realistic, affordable ones). Work in small groups if working as a large group doesn't elicit the best ideas.

Once you have some ideas on the table, discuss them in more depth. Two or three strong options will emerge. You are looking for a single idea which can be implemented quickly and will give people the sense that things are changing. You may also discover one or two other ideas which need more work or will take time to implement but which will, over the longer term, change fundamentally the way the two teams work together.

Finally, don't leave this meeting until everyone is clear about what has been agreed, who is responsible for what and how to monitor progress. Representatives from both teams should leave with action steps. Ideally, you will also schedule another meeting in a month or six weeks' time to review, expose further conflicts and go through the process again. At the Canadian bank RBC they designed a series of Leadership Dialogues which they held regularly throughout the year in order to bring executives from different parts of the organization together. The idea took off and other leadership groups at different levels within the company started meeting to air and resolve conflicts.[2] Once you demonstrate progress with one team you may be able to roll the idea out to different parts of the business which cause you difficulty. As they start to see the benefits in their relationship with you, they may start holding such meetings of their own. That's how you can bring about change throughout the organization.

CREATE AN INFLUENCE PLAN

If you don't want to corral your whole team into breaking down silos you could take a more individualistic approach by creating an "Influence Plan". One of the symptoms of a siloed organization, as we have seen, is that you may be isolated from the rest of the business. You don't know who other people are, you don't know what they do, you don't know where they sit and, of course, they don't know any of these things about you.

Because speculation and gossip fill the void created when you lack information, you may have some quite strong opinions about your colleagues in other parts of the business based on very limited exposure to them. You may have heard that Alison in HR is a bit of a Rottweiler or that Lance in Design is difficult to talk to. These rumours may have been reinforced by other people all too happy to regale you with stories about senior leaders they once met or had a run-in with. All of this bolsters the silo. And yet it is based on assumption. Even if the rumours and gut feeling turn out to be justified, you will never be able to influence those people unless you have a relationship with them.

An "Influence Plan" enables you to identify those individuals you need to know better. They may run a department which your team is reliant upon. They may be "secret change agents" – people who wield more power than their position would suggest. They may be great networkers who can open doors for you. They may be people you find particularly challenging to deal with.

Make a list of the people you need to know better. This list may include job titles with no name attached if you don't yet know who holds that position or who takes responsibility for that aspect of the business. Do some research to fill in the blanks.

Now create a shortlist of 5–10 names. Pick 2 or 3 individuals from this list and consider how you might meet them or get to know them better. Also consider what mutual benefit there might be in meeting. You know what is in it for you but if there is nothing in it for them they may not prioritize time with you. Find a good reason to speak to them about something work-related, suggest lunch or a coffee, get a mutual friend or colleague to bring you along to a meeting and make the introductions.

Face-to-face works much better than a phone call or an email. You are trying to build a strong relationship which will develop over time. That is hard to do without ever meeting the person.

Early in my career I had a major clash with a colleague. We didn't get on to the extent that we sometimes argued loudly at work. I decided the only way to patch up the relationship was to go for dinner. Asking my colleague out was uncomfortable, but not as uncomfortable as the first 20 minutes of our work-date. We talked about our families and our education and our travels. After a while we warmed up and understood each other a little better.

The next day the relationship was a little improved, so we continued making regular dates in the diary to meet and chat. We rarely talked about work at the start. It was just about knowing each other on a human level. Eventually our relationship was so strong that, when I took a job 700 miles away in London, he decided to move to the big smoke too. It is a cliché but that was 15 years ago and we are still friends today.

I can't guarantee this strategy will work as well for you, but ultimately your intention isn't to make a lifelong friend. It is to improve your level of influence across different parts of the business beyond your own silo. As a result, you learn more about the business as a whole and can see how your part contributes to the success of the organization. You can see where "blood clots" are forming, cutting off parts of the business, and you know the right people to quickly air the conflict with and resolve it.

John Barnes says that silos only exist because we allow them to. If you change your way of looking at the business and find areas of agreement between yourself and other parts of the organization (or other personalities within the business), the silos start to disintegrate:

" 'Silos' is a mentality, rather than an actual reality. You have to ask yourself what your own mentality is. Are you reinforcing the silos or are you deconstructing them? You deconstruct them by looking for common ground and not confronting on issues where there is competition but issues where there is common benefit."

END THE GOSSIP

One reason silos are strong is that it feels good to be part of something. If you have an affilliative leadership style (you are good at building strong personal relationships with your team), you are good at bonding people together. We know that people come together to fight a common enemy and you don't want the common enemy to be you. Finding a common enemy outside your team (like the team leader of another team) can create a greater sense of unity amongst your own people.

At the same time, it reinforces the silo mentality. While working closely with that other team is important for your success, all that work you did building them up as a foe to be fought comes back to haunt you. For this reason, putting an end to gossip is an important ground rule for any team.

The "no gossip" rule doesn't mean you can't share information with your team about other people in the business, or events and decisions happening elsewhere. Gossip is about sensationalism, speculation, titillation and revealing private information, and is not motivated by a desire to improve the situation but simply by the thrill of being the holder of derogatory knowledge. Where there is gossip, there is a victim. Sharing information is about revealing facts and data, experience and study. When you and your team are discussing information about other parts of the business, you are interested in using that information for the benefit of the business. You are also honest about what information you lack and are keen to acquire. You don't fill in the blanks with guesswork.

Explain the difference to your team and be vigilant in helping them differentiate between gossip and information-sharing. Hold yourself to the same high standard. Where possible, challenge the gossip style of colleagues in other parts of the business and help them refocus on information and problem-solving.

CREATE OPPORTUNITIES FOR CROSS-FUNCTIONAL WORKING

When we explored Frustration 1, waste-of-time meetings, we looked at who to invite to meetings and who not to invite. Little thought is usually given to this. As a result, you often find you cannot make a decision because the right person is not there or you end up making a decision without all the information. Invariably, such decisions do not stick or create major problems later on.

Cross-functional problem-solving

When your team has a problem to solve, consider asking people from other relevant parts of the business to join you. You might invite subject matter experts or people who are going to be impacted by the decision. You might also invite someone who is neutral and therefore views the problem with a less clouded judgement. You might also consider asking someone who has nothing to do with the issue but is great at asking questions or generating ideas. Obviously you don't want to have too many people at any meeting. It becomes unwieldy. But think more broadly about who might add value.

You may get some resistance when you invite people from elsewhere in the business to help you, not necessarily from the person you invite but from their line manager. If your company is very siloed there probably isn't perceived to be much benefit in helping other parts of the business. When the line manager loses one of her people for a morning, or a day, or a week, to help you with something, she may only see the short-term difficulty for her. What happens to all the work that individual was going to be doing for her team that day? What if that team's results are negatively affected because you took one of her people for a day?

Ian Hill had a similar experience when he changed jobs but was invited back to his old department to help them solve a problem:

"Silo working comes from the fact that a lot of targets are dominated by your own silo. It comes back to measurement and reward systems that are focused on an individual's performance not overall business performance. It becomes very difficult for people to step outside of their silos. You may enjoy a great relationship built over years with an account, but once you move to a different role the benefit can be lost to the organization. When a very large account that I had secured and developed years earlier were unsure whether to continue their relationship with the company, it was obvious that I could help revive the relationship, but this required internal negotiation. Although approved there was a caveat which said 'Yes, you can do this but it mustn't interfere with your other work'. It was all about my performance figures versus the greater compny good. You start to care which 'door of the building' the money comes in."

This is another time when you might need to consider the mutual benefit. If people are going to give up their time to work cross-functionally with you, what is the benefit for them? How does a small amount of time invested now avoid a great deal of wasted time in future? What past examples can you think of where involving the other team at an earlier stage would have prevented a big mess later on?

You may need to start by inviting people from other parts of the business only when the mutual benefit is very clear. In time, once you have proven that the strategy works, the link between their involvement and the benefit can be more tenuous (although there must be one, otherwise everyone is simply in the service of your silo rather than the service of the business).

Rotation

At the BBC we had an "attachment" scheme, which meant that you could apply for a job in another part of the corporation on a temporary basis and return to your primary job after 6 or 12 months. The benefit for the radio show which was losing you was that you would return with a broader perspective, some new skills and fresh enthusiasm having taken a break from a job that may have become mundane for you. At the same time, they would recruit a temporary person behind you (also on attachment usually) who would bring their fresh ideas, enthusiasm and open mind to the show. Although it might take a few weeks to get up to speed in your new job, there were few disadvantages. From a career perspective it meant that you were able to dip your toe into different parts of the profession and expand your expertise. You got to know people around the building and you expanded your contacts list.

It surprises me that so few companies have such schemes. It is particularly unusual for more junior people to be sent on "secondment" to other parts of the business.

If possible though, find opportunities for moving your people around. In exchange you open your team up to people from elsewhere in the company. Make sure that the new people have the opportunity to share knowledge gained in their own part of the business with you. Try not to see this as threatening. The new person may have some very useful information about how your team is seen and what problems you are thought to cause. Rather than blame the bringer of the news, use the data to improve working relationships with the rest of the business.

Equally, support your former team-mate in sharing information about how you do things with their new team. If you see this as "disloyal" you will not get the benefit of this rotation system. Remember – it is not gossip. It is information-sharing.

And when that person returns, ensure there are opportunities for them to bring their new experiences back into the team. An initial debrief or presentation might be useful, but you also want to encourage ongoing sharing of learning and insights gained while that person was away.

You might also seek opportunities to work in other parts of the business yourself. One company I work with has a "back to the floor" policy where leaders spend time working alongside their more junior colleagues, seeing what problems arise, experiencing the pressures for themselves and getting a better understanding of how policies from the top impact those lower down. If a 6-month secondment isn't possible, a day a month on the floor within different parts of the business could help you and other teams break down the barriers between you.

Get a mentor

A mentor is someone who has more experience and generally more seniority than you, who can share the wealth of their experience with you. They are usually well connected too, and can introduce you to people, organizations and ideas which you would not have had access to otherwise.

People often choose their mentor for strategic reasons as well as more personal reasons. A mentor should be someone you respect, although they may not be someone you want to emulate. They should be someone who will challenge you and give you honest feedback, but who also recognizes that they are sharing their opinion rather than "the truth". They should be interested in your growth and find satisfaction in helping you.

However, you may also want a mentor who works in a different part of the business from you, someone who can educate you about aspects of the business you know less about. Your mentor may also be someone who is influential and has the ear of the people who make the promotion decisions. And you may look for a mentor with connections outside your company as well as inside. For this reason, people sometimes select a mentor from a different organization or even industry.

The idea is that this mentor broadens your world. Rather than viewing the business from your own small corner cubicle, you start viewing the business from different angles. What does it look like from the corporate social responsibility perspective? What does it look like from the community perspective? What does it look like from the green perspective? What does it look like from a financial perspective or an HR perspective? Not only can a good mentor facilitate your promotion, he or she can also help you develop the ability to "helicopter" above the business. This broader view means you can see how the parts come together as a whole.

SILO MENTALITY – FINAL THOUGHTS

Silos make for an unpleasant working environment. Rather than working collaboratively, capitalizing on the brainpower in your business, seeking to change the lives of customers through your products and services and finding meaning and purpose in your work, silos turn us into tribes, fearful and aggressive when our borders are crossed and our land is invaded. Not only is such an attitude bad for business, it is also bad for our sense of well-being.

One piece of research suggests that that deadly sin, envy, may lie at the heart of the silo culture. Because we are set up to be in competition with other parts of our own business, we cannot celebrate the success of others because it invariably means they have "won" and we have, by implication, "lost".

In one study of hundreds of executives and their organizations over a 10-year period, it was shown that all of us are vulnerable to envy and that this intensifies during times of economic crisis.[3]

Breaking down silos does require some of the practical steps laid out in this section. But it also requires looking inside yourself and asking whether your mindset plays a part in propping up the silos. We are likely to be most resistant to working alongside people we feel threatened by. Certain people just have that ability to get under your skin, don't they? But the research shows that we commonly envy those who have qualities we feel insecure about lacking. When a colleague from another department asks you a question about an idea or a plan which you hadn't thought of asking yourself, it can hurt a little. As a response, we fall into justification mode. We set ourselves up in opposition to the person who questioned our expertise.

Breaking down silos means adopting a different mindset – accepting that "outsiders" may be able to help you run your part of the business better and seeking help across the boundaries rather than resisting it. The more you can look outside your own small piece of territory, the better prepared you will be for any challenge that lies ahead.

It may not feel fair to be fighting this good fight alone. One might hope that people more experienced and more senior would also be taking issues like these seriously. But one of the greatest frustrations with work is that it isn't fair. Or it certainly doesn't seem like "fairness" is a high priority.

So let's look at that next.

Frustration 5:
Unfairness

THAT'S NOT FAIR

The group sits in a semi-circle, eyes directed towards one of their colleagues who is close to tears. She is recounting how she slept in her car yesterday afternoon between sales appointments because her schedule is so hectic that she works into the small hours and catches up on her sleep in 10-minute bursts during the day. She has asked her boss whether he can provide another pair of hands to help with the workload but, despite the fact that he talks about the well-being of his staff as being of the utmost importance, his response was to explain that everyone else is fully utilized and she needs to keep her head down and "power through" this difficult time.

"And then", she sniffs, "he told me to get a good night's rest and everything would look brighter in the morning".

Her colleagues nod sympathetically and a chorus of "That's not fair" rings around the room.

What had started out as an optimistic and forward-looking workshop about leadership and team work is starting to sound like a Middle Managers Anonymous support group. The opportunities for managers to get together, away from their workplace, and talk about the problems they face are limited. Workshops and offsites, especially those facilitated by an outsider rather than another employee of the company, enable managers to verbalize some of the frustrations they feel, learn about the pressures their colleagues are under and develop a bond borne out of a sense of shared experience. I have been witness to many sessions like this where managers, lacking any other forum to discuss problems and seek support, use the workshop I am running to get what they need – friendship, vindication and advice.

And I have the same sense every time.

It isn't fair. It isn't fair that hard-working, dedicated, talented people are struggling to do their work because of tiredness, stress, unreasonable expectations, lack of clear direction, lack of influence and lack of genuine empathy from their bosses.

It isn't fair that the only time they get to talk about how they feel and support one another is on the rare occasion when they are at a workshop or team-building session with their peers.

And it isn't quite right that their best chance of putting an end to this unfairness is telling me about it and trusting that I will pass the message on and exert some pressure on the senior management to take the issues raised seriously.

I learnt early on that the world of work was not fair just by seeing who got promoted and who didn't. It seemed to me that the people who got ahead were rarely the ones with the most talent. High-flyers were either one-trick ponies who could easily be categorized (such as an average news reporter who had a very recognizable radio voice and was always the first choice for voice-over work) or people with friends in high places (such as interns who were the sons and daughters of senior staff) or those whose face fit (such as a new team-mate who quickly sussed the agenda of the group director and was therefore able to espouse the same opinion, much to the satisfaction of his new boss).

But I do not believe that the workplace must be unfair. In fact, I believe that an unfair workplace is bad for business. So why do organizations fail to take fairness seriously? And what can you do if you experience unfair practices and believe there has to be a better way?

In this section we will explore some of the most common unfairnesses and identify some actions you can take to create a shift in values in your business. At the same time we will look at some of your assumptions and beliefs; assumptions and beliefs which may not be helping you cope with the world of work and which need to be challenged and reframed if you are going to have the influence you want to have in the future. I will explain more about what I mean by this next.

BMWS

During one-to-one coaching sessions, I often provide my clients with a 15-minute "BMW" session. This stands for Bitch, Moan, Whine. It can be very therapeutic to get an annoying incident off your chest in a non-judgemental environment.

By talking it through aloud, many clients see a root cause or a solution they would not have thought about otherwise. Although I listen with an open mind, my job isn't to collude with them and reassure them that they were in the right and the other person was in the wrong, but to help the client explore the part they play in this situation and how they can move forward from it.

BMWs are usually about one or more of the following:

- My organization (or someone I am working with) doesn't stand for the same values as me.
- My working conditions are poor.
- The wrong person got rewarded/promoted/thanked/credited.

The reason I remain relatively neutral when I listen to most of this (although occasionally my blood does boil on behalf of my client) is because I genuinely believe there are many sides to the same story. Fairness, or lack of it, is in the eye of the beholder.

Let's look at this in more detail.

Hypocritical organizations

Most companies are not run by cowboys and sharks, who intentionally set out to deceive customers and make off with people's life savings. But in most companies there is a mismatch between what a company says it stands for and what it actually does stand for. Into this category come complaints like:

"They say they put people first but they just stopped our bonuses".

"They say they care about the environment and then they fly a bunch of executives to the Bahamas for a three-day conference".

"They say the customer is always right but they don't give us the authority to give refunds".

"They say they value loyalty and then they sell the company to the highest bidder".

When you are at the sharp end of policies which run counter to what a company has said it stands for, it seems unfair. Leaders are generally quite poor at communicating subtle messages and often do themselves no favours when they have to make difficult decisions which negatively impact people like you.

However, having coached and worked alongside many senior managers, I also know that they tend not to see their own decisions as unfair ... even though, clearly, their junior colleagues are going to believe they are.

We all endeavour to take the evidence into account (as we see it) and make the best decision we can, even though we know there will sometimes be losers. We make a judgement call, often a difficult one, and find the best outcome given that there are various, competing factors. Whenever I ask leaders about an unpopular decision they have made (or even a decision which turned out to be bad for the business), they can always explain why they came to that decision and demonstrate the logic of their thinking.

So, is a decision which seems unfair, necessarily unfair?

Poor workplace conditions

People love to complain about their working hours. It is a highly competitive pursuit, with people tending to "round up" rather than "round down" their total hours and include commuting time and the occasional late night into their average. That is not to say we don't work long hours in this country. The UK has a high proportion of workers who put in 45 hours or more a week. In 2001 the EU average for a full-time worker was 40 hours a week. In the UK the average was 44. Agriculture, fishing and industry are the worst for long hours, with the service sector being less guilty of demanding long working hours. At the same time, the UK also has the highest proportion of part-time workers in Europe. 24% of all employment in the UK is part-time and the majority of part-time workers do this out of choice.[1]

If you are one of those employees who are expected to be present from dawn 'til dusk (or later), or who feel the need to put in the hours in order to stay on top of your work, these statistics are not very comforting. Just because most people do 44 hours doesn't make your 60 hours feel acceptable, does it? However, it also appears that those who put in long hours get something from it – status, respect, a sense of satisfaction, pride, enjoyment. Some organizations are unreasonable. But long working hours (or the building being too hot or the toilets not working properly or the food in the canteen being cold or any other number of working conditions complaints) aren't necessarily unfair.

It may feel unfair that your partner, your friend or your colleague leaves the office before you every day, but I would argue that long hours are a manifestation of other problems and not the problem itself.

Again, what looks (and feels) like unfairness may not be.

The wrong people get ahead

In my second book, *The Recipe for Success*, I identified qualities which successful people seem to have in common, no matter what their field of speciality. I found that successful people rely on a concoction of good manners, political skill, hard work, confidence and talented colleagues to achieve their results. They acknowledge that exceptional talent on their own part was not their distinguishing characteristic.[2]

Many of us have a belief that a very small set of qualities or abilities should be the deciding factor in who gets ahead and who doesn't. We might believe that it is only fair that the hardest worker gets ahead. Or we might believe that it is only fair if the person who wants it most gets ahead. Or we might believe that it is only fair if the person who gets the most sales or reaches the highest target or makes the most profit gets ahead. Just watch any talent competition on television. Votes tend to go to popular competitors or those who make for entertaining viewing. Sometimes the one with the greatest talent wins, but only if they also have other qualities which make them appealing. We tend not to think of this as unfair but as justice.

And we create a top five or top ten of characteristics which should count based, often, on skills we have ourselves. In my family there is a sense that the person with the biggest personality should be the most successful, because we are all rather big on personality. It sometimes comes as a shock to me when someone quiet, introverted and even shy gets a top job.

There are prejudices in business, and promotion decisions are often made without full transparency about the process or the thinking behind the decision. But assuming there has always been a mistake made unless the promotion went to you or your favourite candidate would be just as unhelpful as assuming those in power always make the right decision.

What is unfair to you may work out great for someone else.

FAIRNESS AND GOOD BUSINESS

Just before we look at how you can end some unfair practices in your company and question your own assumptions about what you see, it is worth understanding why a fair workplace is important.

Obviously, if work felt fair, you knew where you stood, what was expected of you, how your success would be measured and what reward you would get as a result, it would be far more satisfying and meaningful to turn up every day, make your contribution and be confident that appropriate rewards would follow.

But does fairness translate into business benefit? Do fair companies do better financially than unfair ones? Unfortunately, the evidence is inconclusive. One of the most thorough textbooks on the subject, *Business Ethics and Values*, does claim that companies with a code of ethics achieved better "Market Added Value" (the difference between what investors had put into the company and what they would get out of it if they sold) and "Economic Value Added" (the amount by which the current investors' income from the company is greater or less than the return they would get if they had invested in something of equal risk) than those without. The authors conclude that:

> There is a strong indication that having a code … and being rated by one's peers as a reputable company are associated with higher and more stable financial returns.[3]

At the same time they cannot say whether ethical business practices are the cause of the better financial results or whether other factors lie behind these results. It is also unclear whether "good" companies are profitable because they are good or whether profitable companies can simply afford to be better behaved than less profitable ones.

However, there is some evidence that treating people fairly saves businesses money. When people feel they are unfairly dismissed they are far more likely to sue. When people feel they are treated with a high degree of fairness when they lose their jobs only 1% sue as compared with 17% of those who believe they were treated with little fairness.[4] Given that the legal costs of fighting such a case can be hundreds of thousands of pounds, reducing the number of cases of unfair dismissal makes financial sense.

Fairness also saves companies money because it is valued more by employees than financial rewards and benefits. People who feel they are fairly treated put in extra hours, take fewer days sick leave and are more supportive of their manager than people who are unfairly treated but provided with added extras like onsite nursery schools and overtime payments.

And then there is the cost to you personally of behaving in unfair ways. In the Best Companies to Work For survey, employees are asked about the values of their leaders. Companies who can demonstrate that they are congruent in terms of their stated values and the behaviours of their top people score more highly. This suggests that your people are looking to you to be fair. With trust in leaders at an all-time low (only 2% of people feel the leaders of large firms are very trustworthy), you can mark yourself out as exceptional simply by bucking this trend. And it goes without saying that work is more satisfying if you feel good about what you do and how you do it.

All this would suggest there is little good reason to be unfair and every good reason to be fair. So how come fairness seems so rare?

Quick Quiz Questions

What would you do? Bill and Bev work in your team. There is a promotion opportunity and both want the job. Bill is smart. However, he is very laid back. He relies on his intelligence and coasts through life. His results are above average but you know he has the potential to be exceptional if only he would put in a little more effort. Bev is hard working and dedicated. She cares deeply about doing a good job but doesn't have a natural flair. She has to work much harder to get results Bill gets with ease.

If you had to choose between them, who would get the job? Do you go for Bill who has the most potential, who is clearly capable of more and who would be popular in the business, even though he isn't particularly hard working? Or do you go for Bev, who slogs her heart out but may be close to reaching her full potential? Some people would say Bill deserves it because of his talent. Others would say Bev deserves it because she works so hard. How can you be fair?

Let's take another example. You know someone in your company is stealing small amounts of money from petty cash. That person is very senior and well liked by the managing director. You have some evidence but it is a little flimsy. If you blow the whistle you could make yourself an outcast. It could affect your future prospects. You may be forced out of the company and may not even get a positive reference. The publicity might also be bad for the company's reputation, especially if a competitor heard about it. On the other hand, you believe what is happening is wrong and failing to act feels like condoning it. What is the right decision?

Or how about this one. You are about to sit an exam for your MBA. You've heard that the paper has been leaked and that some of your fellow students have seen the exam questions in advance. Do you refuse to look at the paper beforehand, believing that you should be judged by what you do in the exam, even though you may look less knowledgeable than your friends? Do you look at the paper knowing that at least it creates a level playing field between you and the rest of your class? Do you bring the leak to the attention of your tutor, knowing this will anger some of your peers and get them into serious trouble? And let's say you had a provisional job offer with your favourite company riding on the results of this test. Would you risk that just to do the "right" thing? What is right?

It is easy to judge other people's reactions to very real dilemmas, but we are all subject to the same quandaries. Interestingly, 56% of MBA students in the USA admit to cheating during the course of their studies.[5] Research showed that cheating by these future industry leaders was seen as the price of success. And if cheating is allowed (or ignored) at MBA level, the same behaviour is likely to be repeated when those individuals take up positions of influence in business. They may consider "principles" as a luxury when compared with other factors like professional success, financial success for the business or commanding influence and power. We all want to believe we would be in the 44% who don't cheat (although while 44% didn't admit to cheating some of those may have lied). But statistically we are more likely to be in the 56% who do.

It is worth taking a good look at yourself before you rush to judge the behaviour of others. The line between what is right and wrong may be very clear to you, especially if you are looking in from the outside and not faced with these decisions yourself. That doesn't mean people who draw the line somewhere else are necessarily wrong.

With that word of warning, it is also important that you do not accept, without question, behaviour or attitudes which you find damaging, unhelpful or hurtful to yourself and others. This is particularly true when you feel such behaviour and attitudes are bad for the business. We have seen repeatedly in this book how a better place to work benefits the bottom line. And achieving it is often less expensive than supporting an inherently poor place to work. Poor workplaces leach money – the cost of high staff turnover and underperforming employees, the cost of mistakes caused by poor communication, the cost of wasted time in useless meetings … we've seen clearly that resolving these problems doesn't cost much in terms of monetary investment, and saves and makes the business money as a result.

If you want to make work fairer as a way to make the business more successful and improve the quality of your working life, there are a number of places you could begin.

CHALLENGE WHAT IS UNFAIR
Seek to understand

If you suspect unfairness in your company, the first step is to seek to understand it. John Barnes, who is a big fan of asking questions, suggests you start a conversation with the people you feel have acted unfairly, to establish how they came to their decision:

"Why not have a conversation that goes 'That must have been a difficult decision to make, to decide between right and wrong there'. I've had some of those conversations lately and you start to understand some of the pressures others are under that you can't see. Did they really have any choice? It might have been a choice between acting a certain way or handing in their resignation. It could be more 'rock and a hard place' than you think."

The idea behind asking questions and understanding the perspective of those making the decisions is not to influence the decision or present an alternative view (at this point) but to stand in your colleagues' shoes. Be honest about how you would have felt if the final decision was yours (remember the Quick Quiz Questions earlier). Keep in mind the information they had at the time rather than the information available now. Often a decision has consequences which even you would not have been able to anticipate. Arguing that they should have known about consequences which they didn't foresee is less valuable than exploring the process and criteria used to make the decision, knowing what arguments there were on all sides and appreciating what sacrifices that person or team had to make in order to get the best outcome they could imagine.

Having these conversations is good for you longer term too, because they reveal more about the competing priorities in the business than you may be aware of. Your company may state in its values that it places high importance on customer satisfaction and that it believes employee rights are paramount. Sometimes, though, a leader has to choose between one or the other. It may not be possible in a particular situation to do both.

It is revealing to know, when push comes to shove, what the real order of priority is. If you discover that, at the end of the day, share price will always come first or that keeping a customer is more important than keeping a member of staff, you will be better placed to understand the process of decision-making in future.

Obviously, it should not take such detective work to discover this. In a perfect world, decision-making would be transparent and people would be honest about the dilemmas they had to resolve. But in our less than ideal world, asking questions helps to reveal the true operating manual of a company.

Challenge what you see

Once you understand, you can see whether a decision or certain behaviour is unfair or whether it is justifiable. If you still feel the situation is unfair, it is time to challenge what you see.

Stephen Covey uses a three-part process – seek to understand, then to be understood, then find a third way forward – in order to influence change.[6] Phase one – asking questions – is your attempt to understand. Having really understood, you now know what is important to the person you are seeking to influence. You know what you agree about. You know where the sticking point is. You can respect their position because you see that they have taken a position intentionally, they weren't just doing a bad job. They were seeking to bring about the outcome they thought best. You may disagree with their means or with the outcome itself, but you can see that there was method in it.

In doing so, you have demonstrated that you are open-minded. You are "influenceable". You haven't waded in with your "truth" but been open to see circumstances from another perspective. This helps build trust. Without trust you cannot influence. Why would anyone listen to you and take your opinion seriously if they didn't trust you? It may take time to build this trust. Listening once to their perspective might not be enough. You may need to develop a habit of listening for understanding before you can attempt to change their view.

Once you believe you have this level of trust you can embark on phase two – seeking to be understood. Being understood is not the same as being agreed with. Someone can understand your view without agreeing with it. So your purpose is not to convince them you are right, but to explain.

You will need to speak in a language they can understand. Consider whether they are "towards" or "away from" motivated and position your argument in these terms. Consider their values and what they prioritize (you will have a better understanding of this because it will have been revealed when you sought to understand their perspective).

I recently worked with a team who wanted to influence their manager. He was a tough guy who had them all quaking in their boots. As a result, they often behaved in a very reverential way in his presence, almost reversing out of his office for fear of his reaction if they turned their back on him. In conversations with him I realized that he was testing out his team, being hard-headed with them to see how strong they were. He wasn't looking for fear from them, he was looking for a good fight. Whilst I wouldn't advise this approach as a way to bring out the best in your team, when the team finally began to understand him they could seek to be understood in a style which would be effective rather than continuing to do what they had always done and getting the same poor results.

The team built their credibility by changing their body language and tone of voice from a submissive one to a confident "alpha male" style, which their boss understood and respected. They took words from his vocabulary, like "win" and "be the best", "first" and "no nonsense" and used them in their conversations with him in order to tap into feelings that would resonate with him. And then they could present a contrary argument about how to win which still had appeal (because it was about winning) even though it recommended a different approach than the one the team leader had originally proposed.

Sometimes the boss changed his mind, giving the team the go-ahead to try something different. Sometimes he stuck with his original view. And occasionally the team and the leader tried to find a "third way", which would take the positives from both perspectives to inspire a win/win alternative.

If you present your argument by emphasizing your personal credibility (the trust between you), tapping into feelings which are important for the other person (clues about which are in their language) and the logic of the argument (the facts which, where possible, are significant to the other person because they help that person achieve an end which is attractive), you will be better understood. This isn't a guarantee that an unfair situation will change, but it gives you the best chance of success.

Whistle-blowing

If you are still unsuccessful, you may need to go one step further.

Speaking out against practices which are immoral to you is always risky. Even if you feel confident that the behaviours or activities you wish to expose are bad for the business or contravene the normal human expectations of employees in the company, you have to balance many different considerations.

Before speaking out, consider the following factors.

Firstly, you have to decide how important the problem is. Is it something minor or is it something of greater significance? You will want to choose your battles.

Secondly, you have to consider the values of the organization and the extent to which this behaviour is within the rules of the game. What we might demand from our inter-personal relationships will be different from what we expect at work. This isn't because our expectations of work are lower, but because professional behaviour is different from non-professional behaviour. For instance, you may bluff when doing a business deal and that might be acceptable. But bluffing to the same extent with your life-partner may destroy trust between you. Even if you don't like certain behaviour, you might conclude it lies within the rules of work.

Thirdly, you have to weigh up the level of support you would get from other people on this issue. Sometimes, even if you are the only one to find an activity unacceptable, you will still want to expose it. Going with the crowd just because you don't trust your own judgement is cowardly. But if you know that you will be in a minority of one when you speak out, you will want to take this into account.

And then you have to consider your own values. Do you find this behaviour unacceptable because it conflicts with your values or because you are envious, unconfident, petty or naïve? We may not like how someone else does business. We may believe they are bad at their job. But our desire to reveal their flaws may be motivated by a personal desire to see them brought down a peg rather than purely ethical factors.

Next you need to consider what influence you have in the situation. Does raising it make a difference? Does it change anything? If it doesn't change anything, you may still want to proceed – but with the knowledge that a successful outcome will be that you feel integrity with your values rather than bringing about a change of opinion in others.

If you consider these factors you will also have more clarity about who to speak to. Going directly to the person involved is always an option. But you may feel this will make the situation worse. You may be compromising the anonymity of the person who brought the complaint to you in the first place. You may simply anger the individual and encourage him to fight back at you, with destructive results. You may push him further underground and make his behaviour less easy to detect. Or you may be able to convince him to stop what he is doing or confess to a higher authority.

An alternative is to raise it discreetly with someone more senior than you in the business. This was the option taken by Lieutenant General Claudia J. Kennedy, the first female three-star general in the US Army, who reported a fellow officer for cheating on a paper at a professional army school. Dealing with the incident quietly yet professionally, her reputation was not damaged and she continued to progress in her career. You may not find everyone takes the issue seriously, but don't be put off if the first person you talk to seems disinterested in your story. They may need more information. They may need the implications to be spelt out. Or they may need to know that other people in the business take it seriously. Seek someone who will listen.

Finally, you have the option to go to an external source. The obvious one is a newspaper. Beware though. As a former journalist I can tell you that speaking to a newspaper before you have attempted to resolve the issue in less high-profile ways can be negative for everyone, including you. Newspaper journalists are looking for a good story. If they can be seen to be fighting for justice, so much the better. But justice isn't their prime motivator. Once the story becomes old news, your situation may not have been resolved but the newspaper will have finished with it. They do not tend to help you win your case once the story has run its course. You may consider talking to your union, to the police or to another regulatory authority if the problem warrants such an approach.

A difficulty for whistle-blowers (or would-be whistle-blowers) is that they are often implicated themselves. Unless you are brand new to the company, you have probably been working within the system for some time. Having the courage to speak out may mean your past decisions and behaviours attract unwanted attention too. At the least you may be labelled a snitch or an informer. At worst you are seen as a hypocrite.

Of course, whistle-blowing does sometimes achieve very positive ends. Psychologist Howard Gardner puts it very well:

> You need to decide what path you are on. There are so many ways in which the world could spiral either up towards health and a decent life for all or down into poverty, disease, ecological disaster – even nuclear warfare. If you are in a position to help tip the balance, you owe it to yourself, to your progeny, to your employees, to your community, and to the planet to do the right thing.[7]

CHALLENGE YOUR ASSUMPTIONS

Sometimes you can't influence the company culture. Sometimes the unfairness you see doesn't warrant whistle-blowing. Sometimes, even though you have sought to understand the motivations of others and have taken all the right steps to find a third way forward with them, you haven't been able to convince them to behave differently in future. You want to remain in your job but you want an end to the sleepless nights where you wrestle with what is fair and what is not.

How else can you deal with unfairness in your workplace?

Accommodate values

It can feel like we need to sell our souls in order to achieve success in the corporate environment. I have coached many high-potential managers who are concerned about taking the next step up the hierarchy because of the perception that they need to sacrifice their morals in order to operate at that level. They don't want to become just like the leaders they accused of unfairness when they were working their way up.

But do you necessarily have to compromise who you are and what is important to you, overlooking the unfairness you see around you, if you want to succeed? Ian Hill is aware of the challenge. As a relatively senior manager, considering his career future, he wonders whether there will be a ceiling, given his views about big business culture:

> "I'd like to run the UK operation – you can be a force for good, you can have an impact, it is manageable. I don't want to go beyond that into the ruthless world of corporate life. Anything higher than that and you risk becoming too focused by the stock market performance rather than the people who achieve them."

Karen Mellor faced the same conflict as she worked her way up the hierarchy. She does feel she has changed as a result:

> "There is some sadness about having to change myself to fit. In the corporate world you have to play along to some extent. In the business hierarchy you are supposed to understand the culture and live within this bubble which is the culture. To an extent you have a business suit on and your wings are clipped."

However, I would argue that what most leaders do, rather than compromise their values, is "accommodate" other people's values and the values of their organization.

For instance, despite the feelings of sadness Karen admits, she has continued to pursue promotion when the right opportunity arose and feels that she is able to make a more significant difference to her organization the more senior she becomes. She has found ways, by and large, to adapt her style to the needs of the senior management culture without letting go of everything she believes in.

In considering how far up the organization you want to go, values are clearly a factor. As a junior manager, you are close to the ground. You can see the direct impact of the decisions you are making and tend to make decisions on a case-by-case basis. However, as you move up the organization, decision-making can become more complex. You are not just considering what is good for you or your team. You are considering what is good for you, your team, your company, even the national economy. Depending on your industry, you may be taking into account the impact on the environment, on the local community, on political stability and the health and well-being of the population.

In such situations there are always pay-offs. It may not be that you have to sacrifice your values, but that your values are really tested. It is easy to be high and mighty from the sidelines. But with many competing needs and priorities, what do you really believe?

Many middle managers would rather not know. They would rather, understandably, keep life relatively simple. And if this feels right to you, you may agree with Ian Hill that there is a mid-level of responsibility that requires you to grow but doesn't require you to put your values under such pressure.

However, if you are keen to put your values to the test, you will need to shift the way you view values. It is something John Barnes is aware of. He appreciates the sense of conflict one can feel when operating within the corporate moral maze but has found a way to adapt, without compromising his sense of right and wrong:

"I understand how people can feel because I had similar feelings myself when I was more junior. But I learnt to accommodate values, to view values as a mechanism to understand the culture as opposed to principles you can't negotiate. I thought 'values' were the same as 'principles' and I had to have strong principles. However, a value like 'Integrity' is a continuum, not an absolute. I gravitate to people who have more integrity than someone whom I perceive as lower down that continuum. But just because someone might have lower integrity to me, that doesn't mean they don't share my values. You have to establish where you are in relation to the other person and work with that."

Is there a difference between accommodating values and sacrificing values? Yes, but where that line is drawn will be different for each person. One test is to ask yourself, "If my behaviour was published in the newspaper for everyone to see, how would I feel?"

If you could justify the thinking behind a decision or a way of behaving in your own mind, even if you admit it was unpopular, you are probably still operating within your values. If you would be mortified and have no counter-argument to explain what you and your organization did, you have probably stepped over a line.

A decision can be unpopular and still be the right thing to do. However, you must know why you supported it. I occasionally run media training sessions for senior leaders who may need to speak to the press if a story about their business hits the headlines. Sometimes they need to explain decisions they have taken to an aggressive and point-scoring journalist. Their initial response in our mock-up interviews is to avoid the question or answer a question which is not being asked. They might say:

"That's not really the right question. The right question is ..."

However, this simply gives the impression that the interviewee does not have a good argument for his behaviour. In reality, this is rarely the case. The argument may be complex but there is one. Instead, I ask delegates to prepare an explanation which they truly believe. The journalist might not like it. But the audience will appreciate their honesty. An example is:

"We've done as much as we can to limit the number of job losses. We know that this is going to hit some parts of the population hard but we are working with community leaders to find ways to minimize the impact ..."

The same applies in the workplace. If you can't "show your workings" – the method you went through to make a certain decision – and you can't live by that process, you probably have sacrificed your values too much.

Walk the talk

One of the greatest challenges as a leader-manager is to look at yourself in the mirror with the same critical eye as you look at other people. Most leader-managers are hard on themselves. They have high personal expectations and they often find fault in their own work even if other people find it exemplary. So you may feel you are even more critical of yourself than you are of other people.

The kind of "self-criticism" I am talking about is something different. I mean, do you really see who you are, how you impact others and whether what you say and what you do are aligned? In the Mis-Leadership section we explored authenticity and covered how our words and actions need to be consistent in order for other people to willingly follow.

If you feel your workplace is unfair, you may need to look closer to home first. Do people in your team feel you are fair? If you aren't sure, you need to ask them.

Find out how the decisions you have taken are working on a day-to-day basis. Are there winners and losers? The losers may feel the decision was unfair. Have your decisions been misinterpreted? If so, you may not have been clear about the thinking behind the decision and therefore some people may feel you made a poor choice. Do people feel "in the dark"? Do they see enough of you and have the opportunity to know you? Do you know them? If not, they may not see the connection between what they are doing and why they are doing it. Again, they may assume you had less than noble intentions.

You may also want to ask trusted advisors for feedback. As well as someone inside the organization whom you respect for their honesty, ask one or two people outside the organization for some straight talking. How do they see your behaviour, your attitudes and your decision-making? Do they think there is a whiff of unfairness to what you do or how you do it? As an outsider, they are not influenced by the culture of your organization and have not become part of the system. They may see more clearly where you are out of sync with your words or your values.

And, be honest with yourself about the beliefs and assumptions which inform your decisions and your behaviours. Are you guided by an outdated set of beliefs (e.g., you tell yourself that high staff turnover just demonstrates how young people today lack a work ethic rather than asking yourself whether high staff turnover means you are leading badly)? Do you blame others and see yourself as the victim? Do you try your best to communicate clearly, to lead convincingly and listen openly, but never seem to get the results you expected?

Psychologist Howard Gardner has a great test if you want to know whether you are being fair or not.[8] Ask yourself what your mother would think if she knew what you were doing? If she wouldn't understand, you may need to take another long, hard look in that mirror.

START SMALL

It can be frustrating when you see a great deal which feels unfair in your organization and yet you can't get to the heart of it and resolve it wholesale. But the leaders I interviewed for this book were keen to tell me about the small ways they had changed their own attitudes or the attitudes of others, or made small inroads into tackling unfairness at work. Their examples might help you focus on the small steps you could take to challenge unfairness in your working environment.

Demonstrate gratitude

When John Barnes took on a site management role early in his career he saw bad practice, poor morale and unfairness all around the operation. But he started to tackle it by showing gratitude.

As a hard-working leader with difficult decisions to make and tough targets to achieve, he was frustrated when members of his team needed so much support, positive strokes and encouragement. It felt unfair that he had to accept and show appreciation for minor gestures from his staff, especially when he didn't require it from his bosses. But he soon began to see the impact it had:

> "A senior manager wants a pat on the back for bringing me coffee? Go and give me a strategy for improving quality in my plant and I might be a bit more impressed! But I learnt the rule of small improvements and I brought that into this newer role, which has made all the
>
> *Continued*

> difference. I had tried all sorts of strategies for engaging my staff, but the rule of small gratitudes moved people further than they had ever moved before. I used to think 'Oh thanks very much. I've got the 1% of the population who only respond to this'. But once you've seen the value of it, you realize there are a lot of people who respond well to this style of leadership."

Rather than refusing to accept what he saw around him, he found a strategy which worked, shifted his perspective (and accommodated the values of his team) and was successful at engaging even the most resistant team member.

Be more politically savvy

Karen Mellor, as we saw earlier, has adapted to the protocols of corporate culture. She knows that there is unfairness in the workplace but has found a way to protect herself from damage:

> "I wish I had known at the start of my managerial career that you can't always believe what you hear or what you are told, and that you have to watch and be cautious. People are often politically aligned and if you take them at face value, you have no idea about what is really happening until you find yourself in a situation where a conversation you've had can be brought up out of context and it can be quite embarrassing. Alarm bells go off now if someone I don't know very well suddenly drops in and asks quite personal questions about people I work with."

Knowing what the environment is like has helped Karen develop effective survival strategies. Although she doesn't compromise her integrity, she also accepts what she can and cannot change and adapts her style to the reality she sees around her.

Operate outside the cultural norms

Belinda believes in the NHS, which has employed her since she graduated from education, but still finds unfairness in the way the institution operates:

> "The NHS is very bad at saying thank you to its staff. One of the magical things about the NHS is that staff work incredibly hard and there is a huge commitment to the NHS. They don't earn much but they work their little hearts out. But it isn't enough to say thank you by sending out an e-bulletin. It isn't enough to put a box of chocolates in the kitchen. We are terrible at that. Good managers get that right. I made huge efforts to say thanks to my staff for helping me settle in, but there is no institutional way. You can't reward staff with bonuses or parties in the public sector."

Belinda has taken responsibility on herself and regularly takes her team out for lunch to say thank you, funded from her own pocket. She also makes time to thank staff one-to-one privately, because there is no institutional system for doing so. Rather than bemoaning the problem, which she is unlikely to be able to fix sitting in middle management in a huge organization, she has found ways to minimize the problem as it affects her own people.

OVERWORKED, UNDERSTAFFED

I want to deal with working hours as a distinct part of the unfairness issue because it has been the subject of so much literature, so many newspaper headlines, and so much dissatisfaction at work.

Clearly, you can use all the advice above to address unfairness around working hours. You can shift your own mindset. You can seek to understand, to be understood and find win/win solutions. And, of course, you can adapt to (or accommodate) the accepted rules of work rather than fighting them at every turn.

However, some of our assumptions and beliefs about working hours and work/life balance need to be explored if we are going to be able to address this particular annoyance effectively.

What is your problem?

I was surprised to find that, of the people I interviewed for this book, very few felt working hours were a problem for them personally. This isn't necessarily because they work a 37-hour week, but because they enjoy what they do and do not desire to do less of it.

The distinction between work and life (as in work/life balance) doesn't resonate for many people. They don't put in long hours because they are afraid to leave the office. They put in long hours when there is an urgent deadline, or because they want to do a good job, or because they like being there more than they like the alternative.

At the same time, some people put in long hours because they are poor time managers, because they believe it will make them seem more valuable to the organization, or because they waste energy on unimportant activity.

Clearly, some people do have to work two or three jobs to make ends meet. For them, there is little choice about working hours. And some people do work which requires them to be on the job at all times (I am thinking of the military, for instance).

Finally, some companies are genuinely unrealistic about what an individual can achieve, and see failure to reach certain targets as reflecting poorly on the individual and not on the vast job description.

Before you (or your team) blame their working hours on unfairness, consider honestly which category you fall into. Are you really there because you want to be (even though it feels good to complain and get sympathy occasionally)? Are you there because you have to be (either because you need the money or it is in the nature of the work)? Are you there because you mismanage your time? Or are you there because you aren't confident enough about seeking work which fits with the lifestyle you desire?

I remember leaving my office, when I worked in the corporate world, to grab a sandwich and a drink which I would then eat at my desk whilst checking emails and wondering where all the people taking their lunch at the restaurants and pubs around our office worked. I would see people pottering around the clothing stores and having a leisurely coffee and think "They can't all be on holiday".

Indeed, they probably were not. They just had jobs that gave them a break, or that allowed them to work flexibly, or that were manageable within daylight hours. These days I run my own business and sometimes find myself amongst them, drinking a coffee or having a long lunch, so I know it is possible. If you work for a company which believes it has bought your weekends, your evenings and your holiday time, and you no longer like it, there are options. It may feel like you have no alternative but I can reassure you that there are plenty of people who find ways to work flexibly, work part-time, work sporadically when they need cash, or just do work which starts at 9.30 and finishes at 5.

If you would not consider leaving your job for something with less demanding working hours, you are making a choice. The working hours may be taking a toll, but there is likely to be a greater purpose which motivates you. Most of us can do something about our working hours, if we choose to, and we'll explore what now.

Use your time wisely

As a leader-manager, you need clarity about what is important. As we saw when we looked at Blurred Vision, you need to know what your team does, how it contributes to the business and what the priorities are.

Knowing what you and your team-mates do all day, and whether too much time is spent on high-effort, low-return activities, is fundamental to understanding whether you are working on the right stuff. A great deal of time is wasted (and long hours follow) when teams spend time on urgent non-important tasks which do not take us closer to the big vision. If you suspect time is not being well managed, consider the following.

Activities which you prioritize should be "important" – they enhance relationships and accomplish results. Into this category go planning and anticipating problems ahead, building relationships (trust, networking, living by values), maintenance of equipment and taking care of personal well-being. These activities are not necessarily urgent, although if they are left undone, they become urgent and important.

The more time you put into non-urgent important activity, the fewer crisis and last-minute deadlines there will be. However, because they are not urgent, it takes dedication to get non-urgent important tasks done, to carve out time in a seemingly busy schedule. People will say "Let's wait until things calm down before we do our five-year strategy" or "I'll get back into the gym once this busy period is over".

Of course, the busy period never ends if every activity is urgent. The enemy of good time management is urgent non-important tasks. And, surprise, surprise, these urgent non-important tasks tend to be the huge frustrations of work – some meetings, interruptions, some phone calls, some emails … People do them because they are urgent but never take the time to ask whether they are important.

Review how you and your team spend time and identify the urgent non-important activities. Find ways to avoid doing them or make them valuable and important. See if you can delegate them to a more appropriate person or team (it may not be important for you but it might be important to someone else), or find a way to resolve the problem once and for all so it never needs to be done again (for instance, if you spend a lot of time dealing with spam, find a good system for reducing junk email).

Get organized

Some people find this easier than others. They are naturally structured in style and can always find their paperwork, have a supply of paperclips and can close the drawers of their desk with ease. If you aren't one of them, get some help.

There is nothing cute about being disorganized. I can guarantee it annoys your team and probably other people in your company. When you are late as a result of losing a report, or because you lost your day-planner or because you ran out of petrol on the way to the office, people interpret your behaviour in countless negative ways. It is bad for trust. And if you are going to change anything about your organization, you will need trust.

Disorganization lies behind many BMWs I hear about unfairness. Not only do disorganized people complain about their working hours, but they often complain when more organized but less talented people are put in charge of projects which they feel they would have been better suited for ("I've run that event ever year for the last five years. Why are they giving it to her this time?"). They complain when deadlines are set because those deadlines always seem unfair ("It's almost as though they want me to fail"). They complain when they are penalized for minor infractions ("I am never more than ten minutes late. I only ever miss the introductions, never anything important").

Make sure this isn't you. Other people in your organization (or outside) will be able to help you clear out your desk, get a good diary system, book your appointments, even sort through your emails. It may be embarrassing to admit you struggle with this, but it is more embarrassing (and detrimental to your enjoyment of work) to be disorganized and manage time poorly.

Recognize counter-productive patterns

I once knew a very capable, ambitious man who came to work in the UK from Australia. His new boss in the UK noticed his work ethic and, possibly unfairly, tapped into it. As an ex-pat he had few friends in the country, so no reason to leave the office at 5pm. When he eventually spoke to me he was feeling lonely, homesick and disconnected from work. Eventually he went back home and took a more junior job. He now says his life is richer, despite the fact his pay packet is lighter.

Your manager may be capitalizing on your willingness to work hard. You may be rewarded for this financially and with more responsibility. And it may be worth it to you. However, it may not be. Setting some boundaries around how you work and what you are willing to take on is important if you want to be successful over the long term.

People do burn out. They lose their passion for their company. They become resentful. What was working for them starts to work against them. Project forward three or five years. Do you still want to be working this way by then? If not, what is going to change? If you don't change it, how can you expect it to be different? Your boss is unlikely to demand you cut your working hours, even if she can see it is taking its toll.

If you suspect your unfair working hours have become habit rather than necessity, take a break. A two-week holiday may be enough to assess whether your hours are just part of the job or whether you are stuck in a groove.

Other unfairness frustrations

"Working hours" deserves its own space in this section about unfairness because it is such a widespread issue. However, there are plenty of other everyday unfairnesses which you may want to explore in more depth. You may feel your company is particularly unfair in the way it rewards some staff. You may feel your company is particularly unfair in the way it deals with poor performance. You may feel your company is particularly unfair in the way it treats working parents or the way it treats workers who don't have families. But the same principles apply.

Ask yourself honestly what the real frustration is. Ask yourself whether you have done everything you can to influence the policy. Ask yourself what part you play in this unfairness. And, of course, ask yourself whether you really need to put up with it or whether you have alternative options.

UNFAIRNESS – FINAL THOUGHTS

Fairness is not a science. It is an art. As with all art, there will be great debate about whether your work is genius or something a five-year-old could have done with their eyes shut. You are not going to please everyone. However, given that you will always have to make pay-offs, how do you ensure that you've done the best you could with the options you had?

It all comes down to openness. You must be open to the input of others. Employees want to feel they have been able to contribute to the final decision (even if you did not act on their advice). If you are not seen to listen to their input, you can be accused of unfairness.

You must be able to show how decisions were made. Were you consistent? Did you base them on accurate information? Is the decision-making process transparent? If not, people will suspect underhanded behaviour.

You must behave respectfully, you must listen, you must empathize. You must be open-hearted not just open-minded.[9]

If you are open, you can bring about much more controversial changes than your people would accept otherwise. If they know what you are doing, why and what you expect from them, they can follow you. They can see you know where you are going.

"No news" is the worst kind of unfairness. It doesn't give people the opportunity to take responsibility for their actions. They have no time to prepare their mindset. And they can't follow because they don't know where you are going.

But you can be open even when there is no news. You can explain to people what the process of decision-making is and, if you don't know, what you are doing to find out. You can tell people what you don't know. You can tell people when you hope to find out. You can tell people what you are doing to prepare for the unknown and help them prepare too.

In this section we've looked at fairness, and unfairness, from a variety of different perspectives. You will have to choose which approach is most appropriate given the nature of the unfairness you see around you.

But, if you are open, no matter how thorny and unpopular the issue, people will respect you even if they don't agree with your decision. And that means when you look at yourself in the mirror and ask, "Who is the fairest in all the land?" you will be worthy of the response, "I am".

Final Thoughts:
The Real Work

"I don't think we are all being honest."

There is silence around the room as everyone turns their gaze to the speaker. Margaret has been sitting in the meeting room for the last 45 minutes. Not that you would know. She has said nothing. Until now.

"I think some of us are saying what we are expected to say and not what we really feel. I have held back from speaking because I was worried about upsetting you all. But I can't be quiet any more. We've got to say what we really think. I'll start."

That was the turning point of the meeting. And it was also a turning point for Margaret. Seen previously as a sweet woman who always remembered who took sugar in their tea and what the names of your children were, she emerged that day as something of a star. Her ability to whip off the mask that so many of us wear in the workplace and challenge us to speak straight changed the way we operated as a team. It gave us permission to do the same – to call one another on behaviours which were counter to getting results.

Together we have been exploring what makes work feel like such hard work – how organizations seem to be structured to waste our time, how days are filled with meaningless form-filling, how little thought is put into what is really important for the good of the business, the customer and the employee, and how many obstacles there are to talking about these frustrations let alone changing them.

At the same time, we've also seen how a few leader-managers operating at junior, middle and senior levels in their businesses have questioned these accepted ways of working, rewritten the rules of work and taken subtle or even bold actions to transform the lives of the people who work for them. In doing so, they have also improved the customer experience and the profitability of the business.

It isn't easy. If it were, everyone would be doing it. It requires not just a keen eye for what isn't working at work but the honesty to look at oneself and ask, "What part do I play in supporting a system which is so flawed?"

When we walk through the revolving doors of our workplace we don a mask. That mask can take many forms. Margaret wore a mask of silence. I discovered later that this mask was her protection from criticism. She had conditioned herself not to speak out at work because then she couldn't be held accountable. If something went wrong the blame would never stick to her.

I've seen other masks too. The mask that portrays you as the all-knowing expert. This mask is a form of protection too. It prevents other people seeing that you are unsure of the right answer. It may also keep competitors at bay. If people think you are the expert they won't challenge your authority.

Some people wear a mask of confidence. They sing their own praises without championing the talents of their colleagues. This mask sometimes hides "fraud syndrome" – the sense that sooner or later someone is going to realize you don't deserve to be as successful as you are.

And there is the mask of concern. This mask presents you as the one who really cares, who is just looking out for everyone's well-being. And this mask can be a protection mechanism too, diverting people away from difficult, uncomfortable conversations or from actually resolving problems because they are so caught up in sympathizing.

We wear a mask to protect ourselves from threats in our environment. It isn't surprising that, when we enter the bear pit that the workplace can sometimes be, we need some armour. Who wants to show their vulnerabilities, their fears, their insecurities, their mistakes or their distrust of people with more power when doing so may result in being criticized, taken less seriously, seen as a trouble-maker, seen as negative and unsupportive, or even ending up on a black list heading towards demotion, redundancy or even dismissal?

The mask helps us disguise our fears – whether that is a fear of being found out, or of being wrong, or of failure, or of being relied upon, or of intimidating others, or of being disliked, or disrespected, or of being right, or being too successful, or of showing other people up, or of making too much work for ourselves, or of over-promising and being unable to deliver, or of letting people down, or of disappointing people, or of being thought of as stupid, or disloyal, or a poor team player, or a bad fit in our organization, or of being different ...

The problem is that, whilst we are focused on protecting ourselves and hiding our fears, we are not being all we are capable of being. We are, as my Dad often says, "Hiding our light under a bushel".

And it isn't just you. When the majority of people in your organization hide their light under a bushel the lost potential to that organization is huge.

And that is really what is wrong with work.

People rightly see all sorts of problems with the way we work today. We don't spend our time productively, wasting large chunks of it in meetings. We are desperate to learn from leaders who can help us become great leaders ourselves but look above and see few people we would want to emulate. We want our work to have meaning and we want to feel we are part of something important but we don't trust the high-minded values our company espouses and we don't know what we are all working towards. We want to solve problems, to improve the quality of the products and services we offer, to pool our brainpower and see just what we are capable of, but we're kept isolated from our colleagues in other departments and other buildings. And we want to work for companies that care about us and treat us right but constantly see behaviour that is unfair and inconsistent.

All the problems covered so far could be resolved if we were confident enough to remove the masks we wear at work and share everything we had to offer. If we didn't feel forced to limit ourselves, we would be able to assist our company in looking honestly at the challenges it faces in the marketplace and the challenges it faces internally and generate original, fresh, effective ideas to anticipate and avoid them or resolve them when they did occur.

That is not the current reality. People's fears inform their behaviours. They even inform their opinions. Someone who fears being judged will not only resist feedback but will attack the person who gives them feedback, accusing them of trying to hurt them, or demean them, or get them out of the business because they are a threat.

You cannot resolve what's wrong in your workplace if you are dealing with your fears every day. If you hold back from being your true self, from offering everything you have to give, you simply reinforce the culture that says this is acceptable, this is normal, it will never change.

John Barnes has a saying – "What we permit, we promote". If you keep your mask on and fail to challenge the masks you see around you, you effectively prop up a system which you disagree with. You don't necessarily do it in your words. But you do it in your behaviour.

FIGHT OR FLIGHT

Fear isn't always the overt kind of trepidation some people experience when they have to give a presentation, or makes a sales call or make someone redundant. Sometimes it is just a subtle niggling feeling you are barely aware of, a feeling that it isn't wise to be yourself, to be totally honest, to share your gut instincts.

But what happens when we experience fear is that the amygdala, that ancient part of the brain which helps us process our emotions, clicks into action. We experience the flight or fight response which, in the days when we were preyed upon by woolly mammoths and saber-toothed tigers, was a pretty useful response. It still has value but rarely in the workplace. It doesn't help us much when we are trying to deal with most workplace challenges. The amygdala doesn't help you process information rationally and make good decisions about how to react.

When your adrenaline is pumping and your body is in fight or flight mode, you experience stress. Long-term stress leads to poor performance and, eventually, health problems.

All of this cannot be positive in a leader-manager. The issues of the workplace and of business are complex. They require clear thinking, open-mindedness to other opinions, the ability to absorb information, the sensitivity to pick up on the emotions of other people and adapt your style to communicate to a varied audience, the patience to teach, the patience to listen and the ability to act on all of that information in a timely manner.

That is why it is so important to face and overcome whatever stops you from addressing the problems you see around you. I cannot get inside your head, so I cannot guess what those fears are for you. I am sure they are very real. And I am sure that there are risks if you attempt to bring about change. It is up to you to judge whether those risks are worth taking. But chances are they are not as great as they feel.

WORST-CASE SCENARIO

When you are nose to nose with a grizzly bear you are probably pretty accurate about the dangers you face. Mauling is a very real possibility. But the dangers we face at work are less simple to categorize. When you are nose to nose with your line manager, thrashing out whether the team's priorities really make sense given the needs of the business at this time, it will certainly feel dangerous, but exactly what the danger is will be less clear.

As we have seen, people have different fears which inform their decisions about how to behave. But there are real risks if you want to bring about change. You have to recognize what those risks are and whether they are worth taking.

In making this calculation, don't let the amygdala get to work. Calmly consider the possible outcomes if you begin to address the problems you see around you. We often jump to "worst-case scenario" when we consider the risks, but that is only one possible outcome of trying to bring about change in your business or in your team. It is also possible that you will be successful.

In order to judge, start by listing all the concerns you have, even the ones that seem irrational. Consider:

What are the risks to me?
What are the risks to others?
What are the risks to the business?

Then consider the likelihood of those risks coming to pass.

People often worry about being seen as a trouble-maker and eventually losing their job. This risk may seem too great if all you want to do is get better food in the canteen. It's not worth losing your job over. So when you consider "What are the risks to me and it is worth it?", you may conclude there is a potentially devastating risk and it would not be worth it. However, would you really get fired for speaking out about that issue? What is the likelihood of that risk coming to pass? In most companies the chances are low.

Next, consider how to minimize the risks you have identified.

One risk is that you upset someone. So think about how you could speak out and yet still take care of the vulnerabilities of other people. This might include developing a stronger relationship of trust with this person before talking to them about the issue. It might include finding the right time rather than speaking to them when you see them in the corridor. How else might you minimize the risk?

Finally, consider whether you can live with the consequences if one of these likely outcomes cannot be avoided.

If you have established the risks and the likelihood of them coming to pass, and, where possible, you have sought to minimize those risks, you have to ask whether you are willing to handle the fallout. Even if you do everything "right", people might not like what you have to say. They may be hurt. They may disagree. They may change their opinion of you. And you may decide that is acceptable. Just because you are acting in good faith and doing what you believe to be right, doesn't mean you will be popular, applauded or agreed with. But you may still feel the issue is worth speaking up about and trying to fix for the greater good.

And what is the worst that can happen?

On the very rare occasions I am aware of that someone did lose their job (not necessarily immediately but eventually) because they were an outspoken or proactive employee, the outcome is never the end of the world as we know it. In most cases, when one door closes another five doors open. Being forced out of a business (which is most people's worst-case scenario) is often an opportunity to do something new, something more in keeping with your values and something which more completely capitalizes on what you have to offer.

IT TAKES TIME

I only mention this because reading about work and feeling reassured that there is something that can be done to change it is only the first step of the process. If your work is going to be any different, you will have to take action. And there are many competing pressures that will make this difficult. If you have ever tried to change your workplace in the past, you will know how quickly you want to give up. After three or four rejections of your idea you may admit defeat. But most great ideas, and great people, experience rejection before they experience success.

Steve Jobs, the founder of Apple Computer Inc., was famously told by Hewlett-Packard "Hey, we don't need you. You haven't got through college yet".[1]

If you face scepticism or even total rejection, feel reassured that it is a necessary step towards transforming the world.

Changing your organization and changing yourself is probably going to be a life-long project. But that should be comforting. You don't have to do all of this at once. You don't have to change anything in a day. You just need to get started.

THE LEARNING CONTINUES

John-Harvey Jones said, "People want jobs which have continual interest, and enable them to grow personally".[2]

Being a leader-manager gives you an unrivalled opportunity to learn about yourself, to learn about others, to learn about business and to understand what really matters to you.

The managers I spoke to for this book were all honest about what they had achieved and what was still left to be done. None of them felt they were experts. They all said they were still learning.

Ian Hill says he has learnt, in his management career, what he truly cares about:

> "As a manager, should I care what my Gallup score is? No. I am more interested to hear the story about one of my colleagues who had a puncture on the way home and the 5 other colleagues who stopped to help him."

John Barnes says being a manager has taught him what his strengths are:

> "The young me would probably think I was a bit boring, a bit risk averse even though I am not. I'd like to think he thought I was quite a good teacher or even a coach and very clear thinking, which I wasn't when I was younger. I am not sure I would have spotted that in those days."

Paul Currah says he has learnt where to focus his attention:

> "The key is to ask, 'What difference did I make today?'"

What you have already learnt in your career to date, and what you learn as you grow and develop as a leader and manager, will be unique to you. What I can tell you is that you will only achieve what you are capable of, and make work work for you and your friends and colleagues, if you keep learning about yourself.

Work can really work. With determined effort we can make it inspiring and fulfilling as well as profitable and successful. We might not change the world but we might be able to change our little patch of cubicles. If you could help take the dread out of Monday mornings for your staff, or get so lost in your work that you forgot to watch the clock or refused to take part in the ritual of complaining about your boss because you genuinely thought he was a good guy, you could certainly say you had made a difference.

So go out and learn, grow, talk to people, listen, try something new today and show what you are capable of. Now, that's work you could get really excited about.

Notes

INTRODUCTION: THE 5 FRUSTRATIONS OF WORK AND HOW TO FIX THEM FOR GOOD

1. Richard Florida and Jim Goodnight, "Managing for creativity", *Harvard Business Review* (July/August 2005), pp. 125–131.
2. Sylvia Ann Hewlett, Laura Sherbin and Karen Sumberg, "How gen Y and boomers will reshape your agenda", *Harvard Business Review* (July/August 2009), pp. 71–76.
3. Hay Group website 2010, http://www.haygroup.com/ww/services/index.aspx?ID=117.

WHEN WORK WORKS

1. Peter Warr and Guy Clapperton, *The Joy of Work? Jobs, Happiness and You*, 1st edition (Routledge, 2010), p. 7.
2. Marcus Buckingham and Curt Coffman, *First, break all the rules – what the world's greatest managers do differently*, 1st edition (Pocket Books, 2005), p. 25.
3. Nathan T. Washburn, "Why profit shouldn't be your top goal", *Harvard Business Review* (December 2009), p. 23.
4. Sergio Marchionne, "First person – Fiat's extreme makeover", *Harvard Business Review* (December 2009), p. 46.

FRUSTRATION 1: WASTE-OF-TIME MEETINGS

1. "Meetings in America", Research by the National Statistics Council, quoted in a Verizon Conferencing White Paper, https://e-meetings. verizonbusiness.com/global/en/meetingsinamerica/uswhitepaper. php.
2. Patrick Lencioni, *Death by Meeting – A leadership fable* (Jossey-Bass, 2004), p. 230.
3. Michael C. Mankins, "Stop wasting valuable time", *Harvard Business Review* (September 2004), p. 62.
4. Patrick Lencioni, *Death by Meeting – A leadership fable* (Jossey-Bass, 2004), pp. 235–249.
5. Blaire Palmer, *The Recipe for Success – What really successful people do and how you can do it too*, 1st edition (A&C Black, 2009), p. 55.

FRUSTRATION 2: MIS-LEADERSHIP

1. Marcus Buckingham and Curt Coffman, *First, Break All the Rules – what the world's greatest managers do differently*, 1st edition (Pocket Books, 2005).
2. Marcus Buckingham, "What great managers do", *Harvard Business Review* (March 2005), p. 1.
3. Abraham Zaleznik, "Managers and leaders – are they different?" *Harvard Business Review* (March/April 1992), p. 1.
4. Mark B. Stewart, *The Quantum Advantage – A new leadership guide for business managers*, 1st edition (Blackhall, 2004), p. 16.
5. Sylvia Ann Hewlett, Laura Sherbin and Karen Sumberg, "How gen Y and boomers will reshape your agenda", *Harvard Business Review* (July/August 2009), p. 76.
6. Marshall Goldsmith with Mark Reiter, *What Got You Here, Won't Get You There – how successful people become even more successful*, 1st edition (Profile Books, 2008), p. 26.

7. Rob Goffee and Gareth Jones, "Why should anyone be led by you?" p. 11.

8. Peter F. Drucker, "What makes an effective executive", *Harvard Business Review* (June 2004), p. 63.

9. Saj-nicole A. Joni and Damon Beyer, "How to pick a good fight", *Harvard Business Review* (December 2009), p. 50.

10. Saj-nicole A. Joni and Damon Beyer, "How to pick a good fight", *Harvard Business Review* (December 2009), p. 50.

11. Daniel Shapiro, "Why repressing emotions is bad for business", *Harvard Business Review* (November 2009), p. 30.

12. Andrew O'Connell, "Hotter heads prevail", *Harvard Business Review* (December 2007), p. 22.

13. Saj-nicole A. Joni and Damon Beyer, "How to pick a good fight", *Harvard Business Review* (December 2009), p. 53.

14. Research carried out by David McClelland, George Litwin and Robert Stringer (1968) from Harvard University and discussed in *Motivation and Organisational Climate*, Harvard University Press, January/February 1968.

15. Marcus Buckingham and Curt Coffman, *First, Break All the Rules – what the world's greatest managers do differently* (Pocket Books, 2005), p. 29.

FRUSTRATION 3: BLURRED VISION

1. John Harvey-Jones, *Making It Happen – reflections on leadership*, 1st edition (William Collins, 1988), p. 29.

2. John Harvey-Jones, *Making It Happen – reflections on leadership*, 1st edition (William Collins, 1988), p. 33.

3. Richard Barrett, *Liberating the Corporate Soul – Building a Visionary Organisation*, 1st edition (Butterworth-Heinemann, 1998), p. 105.

4. James C. Collins and Jerry I. Porras, "Building your company's vision", *Harvard Business Review* (September 1996), p. 2.

5. James M. Kouzes and Barry Z. Posner, "To lead, create a shared vision", *Harvard Business Review* (January 2009), p. 20.

6. Thomas A. Stewart, "What the long term takes", *Harvard Business Review* (July/August 2007), p. 12.

7. James C. Collins and Jerry I. Porras, "Building your company's vision", *Harvard Business Review* (September 1996), p. 9.

8. Richard Barrett, *Liberating the Corporate Soul – Building a Visionary Organisation*, 1st edition (Butterworth-Heinemann, 1998), pp. 121–122.

9. James C. Collins and Jerry I. Porras, "Building your company's vision", *Harvard Business Review* (September 1996), p. 9.

10. Richard Tanner Pascale and Jerry Sternin, "Your company's secret change agents", *Harvard Business Review* (May 2005), p. 1.

11. John P. Kotter, "Leading change: why transformation efforts fail", *Harvard Business Review* (January 2007), p. 98.

12. John P. Kotter, "Leading change: why transformation efforts fail", *Harvard Business Review* (January 2007), p. 98.

13. Peter Guber, "The four truths of the storyteller", *Harvard Business Review* (December 2007), p. 56.

FRUSTRATION 4: SILO MENTALITY

1. Patrick Lencioni, *Silos, Politics and Turf Wars – a leadership fable*, 1st edition (Jossey-Bass, 2006), p. 178.

2. Douglas A. Ready, "How to grow great leaders", *Harvard Business Review* (December 2004), p. 95.

3. Tanya Menon and Leigh Thompson, "Envy at work", *Harvard Business Review* (April 2010), p. 74.

FRUSTRATION 5: UNFAIRNESS

1. Kate Bishop, *Working Time Patterns in the UK, France, Denmark and Sweden*, Labour Market Division, Office for National Statistics,

March 2004, http://www.statistics.gov.uk/articles/labour_market_trends/Working_time_patterns.pdf.

2. Blaire Palmer, *The Recipe for Success – what really successful people do and how you can do it too* (A&C Black, 2007).

3. Colin Fisher and Alan Lovell, *Business Ethics and Values – individual, corporate and international perspectives,* 3rd edition (FT Prentice Hall, 2003), p. 13.

4. Joel Brockner, "Why it's so hard to be fair", *Harvard Business Review* (March 2006), p. 124.

5. Howard Gardner, "The ethical mind", *Harvard Business Review* (March 2007), p. 53.

6. Stephen Covey, *The Seven Habits of Highly Effective People* (Simon & Schuster, 1989), p. 255.

7. Howard Gardner, "The ethical mind", *Harvard Business Review* (March 2007), p. 56.

8. Howard Gardner, "The ethical mind", *Harvard Business Review* (March 2007), p. 56.

9. Joel Brockner, "Why it's so hard to be fair", *Harvard Business Review* (March 2006), p. 123.

FINAL THOUGHTS: THE REAL WORK

1. Guy Kawasaki, *Rules for Revolutionaries: The capitalist manifesto for creative and marketing new products and services,* 1st edition (Harper Business, 1999), pp. 161–168.

2. John Harvey-Jones, *Making It Happen – reflections on leadership,* 1st edition (Fontana, 1988), p. 316.

About the Interviewees

John Barnes

John Barnes is a General Manager for a large manufacturing site in the South of England.

During a 20-year career in manufacturing, he has always managed people in corporate organizations with cross-cultural communications where making sense of the environment around him and his staff is key to motivating them to deliver successful results. His first role was managing a team of forklift drivers and he now has over 300 staff to consider. He says the two roles are quite similar, "It's just that there are now 300 people ready to provide me with expert advice on where I can improve!"

Paul Currah

Paul Currah is passionate about spending money, especially when it's not his own; that's why he's been in purchasing for 20 years. Having recently moved from a pharmaceutical giant to a medium-sized private company, he finds he now has fewer colleagues today than he had managers before!

Paul would love to be known for getting the best out of people, but recognizes that that requires him to get the best out of himself too. Of this challenge he says, "The quest continues!"

Jane Ginnever

Jane Ginnever is Group HR Manager for a group of integrated property services companies operating throughout England and currently employing almost 400 people. It has been highly placed in the Fast Track 100 for the last 3 years.

Jane is responsible to the CEO for the development of people management throughout the Group and also for helping him refocus the business on quality of service and long-term sustainability. She has over 20 years' experience of managing people and operations and has Masters degrees in business administration and HR management. She says the old adage "You learn something new every day" has never been more appropriate.

Ian Hill

Ian Hill is a European Area Sales Manager for an international technology company. He manages a team of 5 across Europe, motivating and challenging them to deliver effective solutions and to get results.

Working in a matrix organization means he reports to a European Business Director and several Country Business Leaders. Ian was 29 when he first had line management responsibility, but since then has had direct and indirect responsibility for over 200 multinational staff. He notes "The variety adds to the challenge and I am always seeking new ways to manage effectively".

Belinda

Belinda joined the NHS as part of a Management Training Scheme. She now works at Assistant Director level. Her name has been changed to protect her anonymity.

Graham Massey

Graham Massey is the co-founder and MD of thehouse, a brand agency that generates excitement and business success by building big visions, defining purposeful brand values, encouraging dynamic company culture and creating high-impact communication.

He has been managing people for 30 years, first in the hotel and hospitality industry and now in his own company. His view on successful companies is "It's what's inside that counts". Employees will connect more readily with their company "brand" if their heart is in it.

"After all", he adds, "The heart is the key organ for measuring what is important to us – if we do something that feels good it lifts. If we do something that feels bad it drops. Companies which involve employees in the future of the business allow them to put their heart into their work and feel they were part of making something important happen".

Karen Mellor

Karen Mellor is Manager of the Business Planning and Operations group of a large pharmaceutical company, focused on the Research Informatics area of Drug Discovery. She is responsible for ensuring the group's portfolio of projects and activities are strategically aligned and managed to the planned delivery schedule.

Her globally dispersed team of 10 line reports manage projects and handle a range of activities to ensure effective and efficient operations of the group. She reports in to the Director of Research Informatics and also provides executive support to his leadership team.

Karen has held line management positions for over 20 years and is, by her own admission, trying desperately to make it more fun. Her keywords are trust and openness.

About the Author

Blaire Palmer is an author, executive coach and behavioural change expert. She is managing director of Taming Tigers, which specializes in helping companies achieve bold, ambitious goals through their leaders and helps leaders get their mindset right for success.

Blaire began her professional life as a journalist, producing the BBC's flagship news programme *Today* with John Humphrys and Jim Naughtie and *Woman's Hour* with Jenni Murray.

Over the last decade Blaire has become a leading light in the coaching profession, playing a pivotal role in influencing how coaching is delivered in the corporate world and beyond. Today she is one of the country's most senior and experienced coaches and creative thinking partners.

She is the author of two other books: *The Hyper-Creative Personality* and *The Recipe for Success*, is a regular guest expert on Jeremy Vine's Radio 2 programme and writes a monthly column for *Healthy Magazine*.

To join the debate about what is wrong with work and how to fix it, go to www.whatswrongwithwork.co.uk. To sign up for the Taming Tigers blog and find out more about how mindset and attitude is the key to a successful business, career and life, visit www.tamingtigers.com.

Index

Index compiled by Annette Musker